BRITISH WILD BIRDS

BRITISH WILD BIRDS

Devised and Written by BRIAN GRIMES

with photographs by: P. Burton, D. T. Ettlinger, J. C. Fuller, Howard Ginn, Frank Greenaway, Geoffrey Kinns, Eric Herbert, Bob Lambie, Don MacCaskill, Alan Shears, Wolfgang Wagner, John Watkins, A. Winspear-Cundall.

TREASURE PRESS

First published in Great Britain in 1982 by
Hodder and Stoughton Ltd

This edition published in 1988 by
Treasure Press
Michelin House
81 Fulham Road
London SW3 6RB

Reprinted 1989

ISBN 1 85051 278 7

Produced by Mandarin Offset
Printed and bound in Hong Kong

Previous page: juvenile Reed Warblers

PREFACE

It has been my privilege to coordinate the work of the photographers who have supplied the illustrations for this book. Hitherto, their photography has not been used for book illustration, although some of the material has been used for projection at lectures on the conservation of birds and their habitats. The photographers' skills, techniques and patience uphold the high standards of British bird photography, which started with the magnificent work produced at the beginning of the century by the Kearton brothers and R. B. Lodge, followed by Oliver Pike, Neill Rankin and others. To-day, the same high standards are epitomised by the work of the incomparable Eric Hosking, whose photography gives pleasure to thousands and who has given unstintingly of his time and photography to encourage a greater interest in the conservation of birds and their habitats.

This book is not intended to be a field guide of British birds, but to portray the charm, beauty and variety of our birds and, by so doing, to stimulate further interest in the well-being of birds – in particular, of those birds whose prospects of survival are precarious because of the destruction of their habitats or the effects of pollution.

The birds illustrated in this book are either breeding birds, regular visitors or passage migrants. The book has been divided into eight environments to enable the reader to associate birds with the habitats where they are most likely to be seen. Readers may not always agree with the allocation of habitats for some of the birds. The selection of typical habitats is difficult because, outside the nesting season, they range into many different environments in the search for food and roosting, particularly during severe winters. Moreover, many species find acceptable breeding conditions in more than one type of environment. There are 171 different species illustrated in colour with detailed descriptions, while some of the lesser-known birds which are not illustrated are described within their relevant sections.

At the end of the book are descriptions of the aims of the principal organisations involved with the conservation of wildlife, which includes the establishment of nature reserves, research programmes, educational courses for teachers and pupils, and the coordination of the work of international bird societies. In the conflict of interests between politicians, agriculturalists and industrialists on the one hand and the essential requirements for endangered species and habitats on the other, long-term conservation policies have little chance of being implemented. Therefore, it is vital that conservation organisations are given the maximum support to strengthen their powers of persuasion to encourage governments to adopt long-term conservation policies. Many short-term policies have often been, and will continue to be, disastrous to wildlife.

Notes on the photographers also appear at the end of the book.

Right: Arctic Tern and chick, centre right: courtship of Black-headed Gulls and far right: Great Tit at a nestbox

CONTENTS

INTRODUCTION

The wealth of the flora and fauna of the British Isles results from their geographical position, the climate and the geology. The resulting landscape has produced a great variety of habitats for birds in a relatively small area. These islands are essentially a part of the European land mass, from which they became detached some 7000 years ago. During the Great Ice Age of the Pleistocene Period there were four glacial stages, and during the second almost the whole of the British Isles was covered with ice sheets, the exception being the extreme south. In the inter-glacial stages, the climate was warm or mild. To-day the climate is temperate, damp and oceanic, with no great extremes. These climatic conditions have existed since the first vegetational period, which was called the Pre-Boreal Period. This was succeeded by the Boreal Period when the British Isles were covered by dense woodlands that extended almost to the peaks of the mountains. Many of our woodland birds, including warblers, grouse, capercaillies, crested tits and crossbills, established themselves at this time – bird populations and varieties of species being usually directly related to vegetational cover, which provide suitable food and nesting sites.

The mountains and moorlands are mainly in the north and west; they are also the areas of the highest rainfall. Lowland moorland areas, however, do occur in areas made up of decomposed vegetation.

Around the mainlands of England, Scotland, Wales and Ireland there are over 400 islands of varying sizes and some are internationally famous as bird sanctuaries. To name but a few, there are the Bass Rock in the Firth of Forth, the Island of Noss with its teeming thousands of birds, the largest gannet colony in the world at St. Kilda in the Outer Hebrides, and Puffin Island off the coast of North Wales, where many of the sea-birds illustrated in this book were photographed.

The plant life of the rivers, lakes and ponds varies considerably according to the amount of silt, type of soil, speed of the flow or the amount of stagnancy. Usually, where silt accumulates a rich aquatic vegetation develops and this provides food for many ducks, geese and swans.

The coastal shores consist mainly of sparse vegetation, but some of the plants do supply some food for the seed-eaters. The marram and fescue grass of the sandy foreshores offers cover, nesting sites and material for nesting; these habitats are often used by herring gulls. The inter-tidal areas are sometimes dominated by eel-grass, which is exposed when the tide recedes and is grazed by geese. The exposed rocks and mud provide crustacea, molluscs and worms for many wading birds.

Heathlands are similar in composition to moorlands, the soils being acid. Heathlands are drier and warmer, however, and consequently there are variations in plant life, although heather is often the dominant vegetation in both habitats. Heathland is also rich in insect life, in particular in dragonflies, crane-flies and damsel-flies which breed in the permanent and temporary pools. The latter occur frequently in depressions after heavy rainfall, because the water percolates very slowly through the hard crust.

Towns and suburbia offer a wide range of facilities to a wide range of birds, particularly during severe winters. Probably the gardens of Britain's suburbia are richer in bird-life than anywhere similar in the world. This is due to a general affection for birds and the national interest in gardening, which produces a great variety of seeds, vegetables and insects, and a diversity of nesting sites. It is in the parks, gardens and towns that most people become aware of the beauty and fascination of birds and the pleasure that their presence adds to life's scene.

Mute Swan cobs

BIRDS OF THE COASTS AND ESTUARIES

These habitats are very varied and include the changing topography of the sand-dunes, the large expanses of mud-flats, and the salt-marshes with their salt-tolerant plants. Such areas provide many birds with safe feeding grounds, where they can probe into the mud for their food. Marram grasses, which are the stabilising vegetation of most sand-dunes, are sometimes occupied by nesting gulls. The shingle beaches, which are made up of water-worn pebbles of various sizes originally derived by the constant action of the sea against the cliffs, are favoured as nesting sites by little terns, sandwich terns, common terns, oystercatchers and ringed plovers. Mud-flats are the result of silt settling in areas relatively protected from wave action. Often, such areas are dominated by eel grass (*Zostera species*) and green seaweed which are grazed by many wading birds and wildfowl. Brent geese consume large amounts of eel-grass. The conspicuous shelduck is a familiar sight following the receding tides searching for molluscs. Mud-flats, however, are best known for their wader populations. The dunlin and the knot provide a most fascinating sight when they fly low over water, wheeling and suddenly changing course in unison. Typical birds of the mud-flats are the redshanks with their distinctive alarm call ('tuk-tuk-tuk') which can be heard over long distances.

The attractive avocets returned to these shores in 1947 after an absence of about 120 years. Avocets need special saline conditions of shallow water over a muddy bottom in order to obtain food, which they achieve by a sweeping side-to-side motion with their delicate curved beaks.

Rocky shores form a large part of the coastal habitats, especially in western Scotland, Wales and western Ireland. Turnstones and rock pipits are two typical birds of rocky shores and occasionally both cormorants and shags are seen standing on the rocks drying their wings after their deep dives into the sea in the search for fish.

Inset above: Little Tern in flight and below: Herring Gull

GREAT NORTHERN DIVER

Gavia immer

They are distinguished from the black-throated and red-throated divers by their black heads and the white spots on their back feathers. They are frequent visitors to Scotland. They breed in Iceland, Greenland and North America, where they are called loons.

LONG-TAILED DUCK

Clangula hyemalis

These winter visitors from Scandinavia and northern Russia frequent the coastal shore of north-east England, Scotland and northern Ireland. The drakes are distinctive because of their long tails, while those of the ducks are of normal length. The drakes measure in length 53cm and the ducks only 41cm. They nest in the arctic tundra. Their food includes small molluscs, crustacea, worms and some fish. The drake has a loud vibrating whistling call and the duck has a low barking call.

Below: a handsome Eider drake

EIDER

Somateria mollissima

They are probably the most numerous of the sea ducks around the shores of the British Isles and also among the best known because of the use of their nest-linings for the making of eiderdowns. Outside the breeding season they usually spend long periods at sea, while in the breeding season they have a preference for rocky and sandy shores, and occasionally for steep grassy slopes. The drake's colouring is very distinctive, but the duck is drab by comparison. They measure in length 61cm. Their food includes molluscs, crustacea and some vegetable matter. The drakes have a 'coo-oo-ar' call, and the ducks a low harsh call.

BAR-TAILED GODWIT

Limosa lapponica

They are mainly passage migrants from Scandinavia and Siberia, where they nest in bogs and marshes. Their closely barred tails are very distinctive.

Left: Eider duck and young
Below left: Barnacle Goose

BARNACLE GOOSE

Branta leucopsis

These winter visitors from the mountainous and hilly regions of the Arctic frequent the cultivated fields of Scotland and northern England, especially the 'machair' of western Scotland and the western and northern coastal shores of Ireland. Their black and white heads distinguish them from brent geese which have black heads. They nest in the tundra of northern Europe and Greenland. Their food consists almost entirely of eel-grass, but other plants are eaten. The sexes are similar in appearance and measure in length 63–68cm. They have a barking call.

19

BEAN GOOSE

Anser fabalis

These winter visitors from northern Europe and Siberia frequent pastureland close to mountain and hill lochs in Scotland and northern England. They are very similar in appearance to pink-footed geese, but can be distinguished by their orange-yellow and black bills and their orange-yellow legs; by contrast the pink-footed geese are slightly smaller and have pink bills and pink feet. The sexes are similar in appearance and measure in length 71–85cm. They have an 'ung-ung' call.

BRENT GOOSE

Branta bernicla

These small geese are winter visitors from Siberia, Greenland and Spitzbergen and they can be observed in large flocks feeding along the coastal shores of eastern and southern England and Ireland. There are two races of these geese, the dark-breasted and the pale-breasted; the latter winters in Ireland and comes from Greenland. Their food consists almost entirely of eel-grass. The sexes are similar in appearance and measure in length 58.5 cm. Their call is a soft 'rrook'.

GREYLAG GOOSE

Anser anser

During the breeding season they frequent the high moors and lochs of Scotland, where their nests are found among the heathers and rough vegetation. The nests are made with heather, mosses and some twigs, and lined with down and feathers. Males and females are similar in appearance, measuring in length about 81 cm. Their food consists mainly of grasses and, in the winter, includes stubble. Their call is a loud and deep 'ung-ung-ung'.

Above right: Bean Goose
Centre right: Brent Goose
Right and far right above:
Greylag Geese
Far right below:
Lesser White-fronted Goose

20

LESSER WHITE-FRONTED GOOSE

Anser erythropus

Only rarely do these geese from the European arctic tundra visit our shores. They can be distinguished from the white-fronted geese by their smaller size, the greater extent of their white fronts and the yellow circle around their eyes. The sexes are similar in appearance and they measure in length 59cm. Their food is mainly grasses and some grain. Their call is a shrill 'ku-yu'.

21

PINK-FOOTED GOOSE

Anser brachyrhynchus

These geese from the rocky hills of Greenland, Iceland and Spitzbergen where they breed are winter visitors to eastern Scotland, eastern England and the Solway Firth. Only rarely have they been recorded in Ireland. They have a preference for cultivated fields, wet-meadows and estuaries. The sexes are similar in appearance and measure in length 61–76cm. Their food includes stubble, grasses and vegetables. Their call is a high-pitched 'ung-unk'.

WHITE-FRONTED GOOSE

Anser albifrons

These geese from European Russia, Siberia and Greenland arrive in the British Isles in late autumn. They range widely along the west coast of Scotland, the west and east coasts of England and the west coast of Ireland. The sexes are similar in appearance and measure in length 60–75cm. Their food consists mainly of grasses and some grain. They have a loud 'kow-yow' call.

Above: the handsome head of a Pink-footed Goose and below: White-fronted Goose

HERRING GULL

Larus argentatus

During the winter months the resident population is increased by visitors from northern Europe. They are voracious eaters and their capacity for eating almost anything edible is responsible for the increase in their numbers. They are located usually along the coastal shores, although there is an increasing tendency to range further inland. The sexes are similar in appearance and they measure in length 58cm. They have a strident 'kyow' call. Their nests are found on a variety of sites, including buildings, cliff ledges and sometimes on the ground, any available material being used for making them. Their food includes fish, molluscs, crustacea, small birds and eggs.

KNOT

Calidris canutus

These wading birds arrive on our shores from their breeding grounds in the Arctic to winter on the mud-flats along the coastal shores. They are occasionally seen inland near water, and some non-breeding birds remain throughout the year. A characteristic feature is the considerable skill they display when wheeling in unison as they fly in flocks low over the waves. The sexes are similar in appearance and measure in length 25cm. Their food includes small molluscs, crustacea, insects and worms. They have a deep 'knut' call.

Juvenile Knot

23

OYSTER-CATCHER

Haematopus ostralegus

These excitable and boldly coloured birds are common along the seashores and estuaries of the British Isles. They have extended their nesting areas which now include moorlands, cultivated fields, river banks and shores of lochs. Their strong orange-red bills are ideal tools for prising limpets and mussels from rocks, and probing into the mud for cockles and worms. Their nests are scrapes in the ground and are often lined with pebbles and shells. The sexes are similar in appearance and measure in length 43cm. Their call is a piercing 'pik-pik' or a liquid 'kleep-kleep'.

GREY PLOVER

Pluvialis squatarola

Grey plovers frequent our coasts, including mud-flats and estuaries, as both winter visitors from Siberia and passage migrants in autumn and spring. A few non-breeding birds remain here during the summer. The sexes are similar in appearance and they measure in length 28 cm. Their food includes molluscs, crustacea, worms and insects. They have a high-pitched 'tee-oo-aa' call.

Left: female Oystercatchers at their nests
far right above: female Ringed Plover
and far right below: juvenile Grey Plover

24

RINGED PLOVER

Charadrius hiaticula

These plump little coastal birds are common on beaches, salt-marshes, and sandy shores. Unfortunately, many of their natural habitats have been destroyed because of the development of holiday dwellings. They are very energetic and are often seen running with brief halts to pick up food. The sexes are similar in appearance; they measure in length 19cm. Their nests are scrapes in the ground and often lined with pebbles and shells. Their food includes molluscs, crustacea, worms and insects. They have a melodious 'klu-up' call.

SANDERLING

Calidris alba

These small plump birds frequent the barren wastes of the arctic tundra during the breeding season; they are passage migrants and winter visitors to our shores. Some non-breeding birds are resident throughout the year. The sexes are similar in appearance and they measure in length 20.5cm. Their food includes molluscs, worms, fish and crustacea.

SCAUP

Aytha marila

These diving and maritime ducks are winter visitors and passage migrants from northern Europe and Siberia; they have bred in Scotland. They are fairly widespread along the coastal shores of the British Isles. In contrast to the colourful males, the females are brown with a large white face-patch. Their nests, sometimes grouped socially, are located in depressions in the ground and lined with feathers and down.

They measure in length 48cm. Their food includes molluscs, crustacea, worms and insects. The males have a 'cooing' note and a low whistle and the females have a harsh 'karr-karr' call.

COMMON SCOTER

Melanitta nigra

These ducks are mainly winter visitors or passage migrants, but a few remain in Scotland and Ireland to breed, and some non-breeding ducks remain off the coast of north-east England and Scotland throughout the year. Their breeding areas are usually near lakes in moorlands. Their nests are made in hollows in the peat, from grasses and down, and are hidden by heather. The drakes are entirely black and the ducks are a dark brown with lighter patches on their heads. They measure in length 48 cm. Their food includes molluscs, insects, worms and some vegetable matter. The drakes have a series of cooing calls and the female a 'karr-r' call.

SHELDUCK

Tadorna tadorna

They are the largest of the British ducks and are found in almost all counties. They have a unique feature in that both the drakes and the ducks have a similar colourful plumage, but the ducks lack the knob which the drakes have at the base of the bill. They have a preference for sand-dunes for nesting, but also use scrubby grassland and pastureland. Their nests are usually well hidden in bramble and tussocks or in holes. They measure in length 66cm. Their food includes molluscs, crustacea, insects, worms and some vegetable matter. They have a nasal 'arc-arc' call.

Above left: Scaup drake; above right: Sanderling in winter plumage; far right above: Common Scoter drake and far right: Shelduck drake

ARCTIC TERN

Sterna paradisaea

These graceful fliers undertake prodigious journeys twice yearly. In the autumn they fly southwards to the oceans of Antarctica and south America, returning in spring. Their nesting colonies in the British Isles are confined to the Farne Islands and Scotland. The sexes are similar in appearance and measure in length 38cm. Their nests are found in sand-dunes and on shingle beaches and are scrapes in the ground. Their food includes mainly small fish and some insects. They have a 'kee-yah' call.

COMMON TERN

Sterna hirundo

These summer visitors from Portugal, Spain and north-west Africa frequent inshore waters, islands and coastal shores. They are distinguished from the arctic terns by their slightly smaller size and the black tip to their red bills, the arctic terns' bills being completely red. They are extremely aggressive to anyone intruding into their nesting colonies, which are on islands, sand-dunes and shingle spits; the nests are scrapes in the ground. The sexes are similar in appearance and measure in length 35.5cm. Their food consists mainly of sand-eels, fish and insects. They have a 'kik-kik-kik' call and many others including a 'keearr' alarm call.

Left: Arctic Terns
Right: a pair of Common Terns at their nest

Nesting Sandwich Terns

LITTLE TERN

Sterna albifrons

These birds are summer visitors
from the coastal waters of
Portugal, Spain and West Africa.
They nest in small colonies on
sandy and shingle beaches, along
the shorelines of the British
Isles, but these are showing signs
of contracting because of human
pressures. The nests are scrapes
in the ground sometimes lined
with small stones. Like other
terns they are often observed
skimming over water in search of
food, hovering occasionally with
their bills and tails pointed
downwards. Their food includes
sand-eels, molluscs, crustacea
and worms. They are the
smallest of the British terns and
measure only 23cm. They have a
'kek-kek' call.

ROSEATE TERN

Sterna dougallii

These terns can be identified by
their pinkish breast feathers
during the summer. Their bills
are black in the winter and red at
the base during the breeding
season. They breed sparsely in
the Farne Islands, north Wales,
on the east Scottish coast and in
the Scillies.

SANDWICH TERN

Sterna sandvicensis

They are summer visitors from the coastal waters of south and west Africa. They are the largest of the British terns, measuring in length 40.5cm. The black crest is a useful identification feature. The sexes are similar in appearance. Their breeding sites usually contain dense colonies and are often associated with other birds. The nests are scrapes in the ground, sometimes lined with dried vegetation. Their food consists mainly of sand-eels, fish, molluscs and worms. They have a 'kerr-whit' call.

TURNSTONE

Arenaria interpres

These birds are observed mainly during the winter along the rocky shores turning over pebbles and seaweed in their search for insects. Their colouring is a most distinctive 'tortoiseshell'. The sexes are similar in appearance; they measure in length 23cm. In addition to insects, their food includes crustacea and small fish. They do not breed in the British Isles. They have a 'tuc-tuc' call.

Turnstone

BIRDS OF THE FIELDS
AND HEDGEROWS

Until the middle of the 18th century much of the agricultural land of this country was based upon an open-field system. During this period the various Enclosure Acts were enacted by Parliament, encouraging farmers in the process of fencing off their land from their neighbours'. This was achieved in the lowland areas by planting hedges. These consisted mainly of hawthorn (widely used because it would not be grazed by cattle), together with mixtures of holly, blackthorn, hazel, elder and field maple, often interspersed with oak, ash and elm – the last is now less evident because of Dutch elm disease.

Many of the hedgerow plants, such as the hawthorn, elderberry and buckthorn, produce berries on which many birds feed, especially the thrushes. The ground layer of plants beneath the hedges is most important to a number of birds including the yellowhammer, the grey partridge, corn bunting and whitethroat, who frequently use this type of habitat for their nests.

On the higher altitudes in the north Midlands, northern England, Wales and parts of Scotland the enclosures are divided by stone walls. There are many commons still in existence, but very few commoners exercise their grazing rights over these areas and most are being used for amenity and recreation purposes. Many of these commons contain large bird populations because of the natural food available or food provided by visitors.

Grassland occupies much of the British Isles since the depletion of the forests. The continuance of these grasses is due mainly to grazing animals. Some areas, since the reduction of the rabbit population due to myxomatosis, have reverted to woodlands.

There are many varieties of grasses, the most common being the meadow and pasture grasses of the permanent grasslands, which include the fescues and poas, *agrostis tenuis* and *agrostis stolinifera*, *Poa pratensis*, *Poa trivialis*, *Festuca pratensis*, *Festuca rubra*. On the rough hill grazing areas in the west and north is found the mat-grass (*Nardus stricta*). This grass is usually on the drier soils; on the wetter areas the dominant grass is the purple moor-grass (*Molinia caerulea*).

Open grasslands are favoured by a wide variety of birds as

A peaceful Somerset landscape near Watchet, with inset above: a Lapwing in flight and below: a Magpie's nest with its canopy of twigs viewed from above

breeding grounds including meadow pipits, skylarks, pheasants, partridges, lapwings and redshanks. During the winter months many geese, including greylag geese, pink-footed geese and bean geese are often unwelcome visitors to cultivated fields, where they feed on the stubble, potatoes and grain.

Below: Fieldfare and right: Jackdaw

CORN BUNTING

Emberiza calandra

These large buntings frequent open farmland and wastelands. Their plumage is mainly brown and streaked, and their bills and legs are pale yellow.

CORNCRAKE

Crex crex

Once these birds were familiar in our agricultural land, often to be heard, if not seen. However, because of changes in agricultural practices, they now only breed in Ireland and western Scotland. They have yellow-brown streaked plumage, with grey heads and breasts.

FIELDFARE

Turdus pilaris

These winter visitors from northern Europe are found in a variety of habitats including downland, open woodlands, farmland, parks and gardens. During severe winters they visit gardens in their search for cotoneaster berries and rotting fruit. Although about the same size as mistle thrushes, their blue-grey heads make identification easy. They return to their breeding grounds in northern Europe in March. The sexes are similar in appearance and they measure in length 25cm. Their food includes slugs, snails, insects, worms, fruit and berries. Their flight call is a harsh 'chack-chack'.

JACKDAW

Corvus monedula

These rascals of the crow family will steal almost anything – not only other birds' eggs, but any objects that take their fancy and which are useless either as food or nesting material. They are widespread throughout the British Isles and frequent a variety of habitats including fields, cliffs, churches, old buildings and parks. The sexes are similar in appearance and measure in length 33cm. Their nests, which are located in holes in trees, cliffs, and old buildings, are made of twigs and lined with wool, the wool often being taken from live sheep. In addition to eggs and nestlings, their food includes insects, carrion, small mammals, berries and vegetable matter. Their call is a 'chak-chak'.

35

KESTREL

Falco tinnunculus

The most characteristic feature of these birds of prey is their hovering flight as they search for their prey. They are widespread throughout the British Isles and they have recently become common in city centres and along the verges of motorways. On a journey from London to Sheffield along the M1 twelve individual kestrels were observed hovering above the grassy banks. They perform a useful function to farmers, as they prey upon voles, mice, rats and harmful insects. The male birds have a blue-grey head and tail and the females a brown barred tail; they measure in length 35cm. Their nests are found in a wide variety of sites, including cliff ledges, balconies on buildings and holes in trees, and they often use other birds' abandoned nests. Their call is a chattering 'kee-kee-kee'.

Left: the distinctive outline of a Kestrel in flight and below: the male at the nest with chicks

LAPWING

Vanellus vanellus

These birds are often referred to as 'peewits' because of their call 'pee-weet, pee-weet'. Although common on moorlands, they are probably more numerous on arable land and meadows. The male makes a number of scrapes in the ground from which the female selects a nest, which is lined with dried vegetation. Lapwings are easily identifiable because of their black and white appearance and rounded wings, and their erratic flight, with many sudden twists and turns. When their nesting site is approached by an intruder, they will feign injury to lure the attacker away from the eggs or young. The sexes are similar in appearance, with a distinctive crest, and they measure in length 30.5cm. Their food includes insects, earthworms, molluscs and some seeds.

Above: female Lapwing settling on her eggs and displaying the brood patches on her breast and left: Lapwing chicks

37

Magpies and a grey squirrel explore a litter basket

MAGPIE

Pica pica

These pied birds are widespread throughout the British Isles apart from north-western Scotland. Usually they are solitary or in pairs for most of the year, but during winter they congregate in flocks. They are notorious robbers and they steal not only eggs and nestlings, but also glittering objects. A characteristic feature of magpies is their bounding jumps from branch to branch. The sexes are similar in appearance and they measure in length 46cm. They are becoming increasingly common in built-up areas and losing some of their timidity. Their nests are located in trees or tall bushes, and are made with twigs lined with mud and grass, and surmounted with a canopy of twigs. Their call is quite unlike that of any other bird; it is a loud, chattering and penetrating 'chak-chak-chak'.

Barn Owl and owlets

BARN OWL

Tyto alba

Although these conspicuous owls are widespread throughout England, Ireland and Wales, they are absent from the extreme north and north-east of Scotland. They are mainly nocturnal, but are often seen at dusk searching for food, and during the winter months will forage for food during daylight. For reasons not understood there has recently been a decline in their numbers.

Usually their nests are found in hollows in trees, derelict buildings and quarries, and they will also become tenants of lofts in barns and specially designed nest-boxes. They eat a wide variety of food including voles, mice, rats, small birds, frogs and fish. The males are slightly lighter in colour; they measure in length 34cm. Their call is a loud shriek.

LITTLE OWL

Athene noctua

These introduced birds are the smallest of the resident owls in the British Isles. They can be seen flying over open countryside during the daytime, especially on agricultural land, where old buildings and trees provide nesting sites. They do not use nesting material. Males and females are similar in appearance with a length of 22 cm. Their food includes insects, beetles, voles, mice, other small mammals, and some small birds. They have a plaintive 'keew-keew' call.

Right: Little Owl
Below: Red-legged Partridge

RED-LEGGED PARTRIDGE

Alectoris rufa

These game birds originated from continental stock and are now more numerous than the native species in East Anglia; they are absent from Ireland, Scotland and Wales. They are found in a variety of habitats including sand-dunes, farmland, downlands, and heathlands. The sexes are similar in appearance and measure in length 36cm. Their nests are scrapes in the ground and are well hidden by vegetation. They have a 'chuka-chuka' call.

PHEASANT

Phasianus colchicus

These game birds originated in Asia and are widespread throughout the British Isles; their numbers are on the increase. Although many birds are bred for shooting on estates, others live a wild life on heaths, farmland, open woodlands and marshy ground with rushes. The plumage of the males is very colourful, but the females are rather drab by comparison. The males measure in length 83cm and the females 59cm. Their nests are usually hollows or scrapes in the ground usually under cover, and lined with dried vegetation. Their food includes seeds, fruit, insects and small mammals. Their call is a penetrating 'kak-kak'.

Cock and juvenile hen Pheasant

WOOD PIGEON

Columba palumbus

These, the largest of our pigeons, are widespread throughout the British Isles and are sedentary. They are pests to the farmers, as they consume large quantities of cereals. However, many of these pigeons have adopted a city life and, in contrast to their suspicious and cautious behaviour in the countryside, are as tame as the metropolitan feral pigeon. Usually they nest in trees (in cities they will sometimes even use balconies), and their nests are platforms of twigs. In addition to cereals their food includes fruit, berries, seeds and scraps. The sexes are similar in appearance and they measure in length 41cm. Their call is a repeated 'coo-coo'.

Above right: Wood Pigeon
Centre left: Rooks roosting in winter and centre right: scavenging refuse

ROOK

Corvus frugilegus

These sociable birds are common throughout the British Isles. They are found in a wide variety of habitats, but have a preference for agricultural land. They nest in rookeries in tall trees and will use the same nest year after year. However, Dutch elm disease has destroyed many of their habitats and they have been compelled to find new sites. Characteristic of a rookery is the cacophony that prevails during nest building. They steal each other's nesting material and many frenzied arguments are the result. The sexes are similar in appearance and they measure in length 46cm. Their food includes insects, worms, seeds, scraps and some carrion. Their call is repeated 'kaa'.

SERIN

Serinus serinus

These rare visitors to the British Isles, usually in the counties of Sussex, Kent and Norfolk, have recently bred here. They have a preference for cultivated land, parks and gardens. The yellow plumage of the males is less prominent on the females. They measure in length 11.5 cm. Their food consists mainly of seeds. They have a 'tsooeet' call.

Left: the rare and unusually marked Serin
Below left: a fledgling Skylark and below right: an adult Skylark

SKYLARK

Alauda arvensis

The most distinguishing characteristic of these birds is their musical warbling song, which is maintained for long periods as they fly high in the sky. Another distinctive feature is their small crest. They construct cup-like nests of grasses on the ground, lined with wool and hair. The sexes are similar in appearance; they measure in length 18cm. Their food consists of caterpillars, earthworms, beetles and some seed.

Swallow and young: the nest is built on a rafter. The bird on the right is ready for migration

SWALLOW

Hirundo rustica

These harbingers of spring usually arrive from Africa in April. They are widespread throughout the British Isles and have a preference for cultivated farmland. There are indications that their numbers are decreasing, possibly due to changes in agriculture. Frequently they return year after year to the same nests, which are located under rafters of farm buildings, on ledges and under bridges. The nests are made of straw and mud and are lined with feathers. Their food consists almost entirely of insects caught on the wing. The sexes are similar in appearance, although the females have slightly shorter tail streamers. They measure in length 19cm. Their call is a 'tswit-tswit'.

YELLOW-HAMMER

Emberiza citrinella

These resident birds are widespread throughout the British Isles apart from the northern Scottish islands. They are usually associated with open countryside with hedgerows and rough grass; only very occasionally do they venture into gardens. They flock together with other buntings during winter. Their nests are on or near the ground, well hidden, and are made of dried grasses and lined with hair. The yellow plumage of the males is less obvious on the females. They measure in length 16.5cm. Their food includes grain, fruit and insects. Their call is a hissing 'chip' and their song is a 'tint-tint-tint-twee', often referred to with some imagination as 'A little bit of bread and no cheese'.

Above: male Yellowhammer feeding its nestlings

45

BIRDS OF THE HEATHLANDS

Heathland once occupied large areas of the British Isles, because it consists mainly of land which is not suitable for agriculture, being acid and sandy. Although it is not attractive visually for most of the year, during autumn with its purple carpets of heather it enhances the British scene. However, improved agricultural techniques, industrial development, the construction of airfields and the demand for timber have reduced the dry heaths to fragments in the east and south of England. Fortunately, some of the best examples of heathland are now National Nature Reserves or designated Sites of Special Scientific Interest, and so their future is more secure.

There is no concise explanation of the difference between heathland and moorland; both have developed from acid and shallow soils, frequently they overlap and heather is the dominant vegetation. However, heathland has developed mainly on the drier sandy and gravelly soils of East Anglia and southern England. Moorlands are mainly on the upland and wetter areas of the British Isles.

Fire plays an important role in the continued existence of these dry heaths. During the summer months the vegetation becomes inflammable and occasional fires occur, which kill the tree seedlings, but the burned heather recovers quickly. If these fires did not occur, then the heaths would slowly revert to pine and birch woodland.

Gorse and broom are common on many heaths. Gorse is often used as observation posts for the handsome male stonechats and these birds nest in the bottom of these bushes. Whinchats also nest amongst the gorse. The Dartford warbler is restricted to the southern heathlands and is increasing in numbers, after the disastrous hard winters of the early 1960s which reduced their numbers to a few breeding pairs. The stone curlew is another characteristic bird of this type of habitat. It has a definite preference for areas without vegetation and with some sand, gravel or chalk for its nest scrapes. The insect populations of these areas are quite considerable, especially grasshoppers, moths, butterflies and dragonflies; the nymphs of the latter are found in the acid pools.

A typical southern heath with inset above: a female Whinchat and below: this photograph shows the young Cuckoo's amazing ability to push an egg out of its host parents' nest. In this case the victim is a Reed Warbler, a riverside bird, but the Cuckoo will do this in any nest.

CUCKOO

Cuculus canorus

These birds, whose call is a welcome harbinger of spring, are widespread throughout the British Isles. The 'cuckoo' call is made by the males, while females have a bubbling call. Although the sexes are usually similar in appearance, a reddish-brown female does occur. Their measurements are 32–35cm. Their parasitic egg-laying habit is well known. The birds most commonly chosen to act as hosts are meadow pipits, dunnocks and reed warblers, the foster-parents' eggs being imitated generally by the cuckoo's single egg. Their diet consists of insects including hairy caterpillars, spiders, and earthworms.

STONE CURLEW

Burhinus oedicnemus

These birds are sometimes called 'thick-knees'. In addition to their knees the most distinctive feature of these birds is their large yellow eyes. In flight their white wing-bars are conspicuous. They are usually associated with chalky and stony habitats.

Far left: a young Cuckoo fed by a Reed Warbler
Above: adult Cuckoo
Left: juvenile Stone Curlew, the adults have yellow legs and bills

HOBBY

Falco subbuteo

These very fast fliers can be
mistaken for swifts as they
manoeuvre in the air in the
pursuit of their prey over the
sparse woodlands of southern
England. The females are larger
than the males, measuring
30–35cm. They often use old
crow's nests. Their diet consists
of swallows, larks, insects and
sometimes bats. Their call is a
repeated 'keek'.

Right: a young Hobby
Below: a pair of Linnets at their nest

50

LINNET

Acanthis cannabina

Although they are gregarious mainly during winter, mixing with other finches in the search for food, occasionally they nest socially in hedgerows and gorse and sometimes in heather. The males have a pinkish breast during summer, which is not always obvious during winter; the females lack the pink colouring. The nests are made with grasses and mosses and lined with wool and hair. They measure in length about 13.5cm. Their food consists of seeds and some insects. Their song is a series of pleasant tremulous sounds.

Above: a Tree Pipit and right: the photographer's hide

TREE PIPIT

Anthus trivialis

These spring and summer visitors to heaths and rough grassland with scattered trees occur frequently in England, Scotland and Wales, although only rarely have they been recorded in Ireland. The sexes are similar and they can easily be confused with the meadow pipits, who occupy similar terrain for both nesting and feeding. However, their songs are different, the tree pipit's song consisting of a loud and shrill 'teea-teea' usually uttered from a tree. They measure in length 15 cm. Their nests are located in tussocks of grass or under bracken, made from dried moss and grass and lined with grass and hair. They feed on insects, larvae, beetles and sometimes spiders.

GREAT GREY SHRIKE

Lanius excubitor

They are non-breeding annual visitors to the British Isles, mainly to Scotland and eastern England. They have grey and white plumage, and black and white wings.

Below: male Red-backed Shrike

RED-BACKED SHRIKE

Lanius cristatus

They frequent hedgerows, bramble-covered wastelands and other bushy places, mainly in the south and south-east of England. Their habit of impaling their surplus food on thorns has earned them the name 'butcher-birds'. The female's plumage is dull compared with the male's blue-grey head and deep chestnut back. They measure in length 17 cm. Their nests are usually located in thickets and are made of grasses, mosses and a lining of hair or wool. Their food includes small birds, insects, mice, voles and earthworms. They have a 'chak-chak' call.

STONECHAT

Saxicola torquata

The male birds are very distinctive with their black heads and throats; the females are brown with black streaks and do not have the white patch on the upper parts of their tails. They measure in length 13cm. These birds were once more numerous but probably due to loss of habitat they are now common only locally. It is characteristic of stonechats to use gorse bushes as song-posts. Their nests are located near to the ground and are made from mosses, dried grass and sheep's wool. Their call is a harsh 'tsak-tsak' which sounds like two stones banging together.

DARTFORD WARBLER

Sylvia undata

These charming birds are confined to southern England; there is some anxiety about their future as heathland habitats are decreasing. They are easily identified because of their cocked tails, dark grey heads and pink-red underparts.

WHINCHAT

Saxicola rubetra

These summer visitors are more often seen in open heathland with bushes and commons. They are similar to the stonechats, but have distinctive white stripes over their eyes. The males are darker than the females, but this difference is not so obvious during the winter. They measure in length 13cm. Their nests are located on the ground in rough grass or under low bushes and made from dried vegetation. Their food consists of insects, larvae and earthworms.

WHITETHROAT

Sylvia communis

These summer visitors from Africa are visually more obvious than most warblers. They are not as timid as the lesser whitethroat and they are common in scrubby vegetation, hedgerows and clearings in woodlands. They measure in length 14cm, which is slightly larger than the lesser whitethroat. Their nests are close to the ground in low vegetation, often in brambles, and are made from dried grasses lined with hair, and studded with cocoons. Their food consists of insects and some fruit. Their song is a strong chatter, usually sung from a gorse bush or a fence post.

LESSER WHITETHROAT

Sylvia curruca

These birds are almost entirely confined to England and Wales, where they prefer leafy lanes, gardens, scrubby commons and copses. The sexes are similar in appearance and they measure in length 14cm. Their nests are located in bushes, hedgerows or shrubs and are made from dried grasses and sometimes lined with hair. They feed on insects and some berries.

WOODLARK

Lullula arborea

They are smaller than skylarks and have a preference for sandy heaths and woodland edges. Their back plumage is brown, streaked with white and they have white underparts and yellow-white eye stripes. They have a sweet piping song.

Far left: Whitethroat male above, female below. Below: Lesser Whitethroat, the bird at the nest has been ringed

BIRDS OF THE MOUNTAINS AND MOORLANDS

It is difficult to define a moorland precisely. The late Professor W. H. Pearsall described moorlands in his excellent New Naturalist Series book *Mountains and Moorlands* as 'almost any open country, especially if it is wild and uninhabited'. Often, there are descriptive words added to moor which indicate the dominant vegetation, wetness and soil, such as grass-moor, which consists mainly of mat-grass (*Nardus stricta*) and purple moor-grass (*Molinia caerulea*). The latter is found on much wetter areas than the mat-grass.

Heather-moors are well represented on the drier areas of our hills and mountains and, where the rainfall is high, heather occupies the steeper slopes. Heathers usually occur to the exclusion of almost all other vegetation. The dominant plant is ling (*Calluna vulgaris*), which is usually associated with cross-leaved heath (*Erica tetralix*), bell heather (*Erica cinerea*) and bilberry (*Vaccinium myrtillus*). These moors are used for game bird shooting and are subject to regular burning to encourage the growth of young shoots, which form part of the red grouse's diet.

Sedge-moors consist of deer sedge (*Scirpus caespitosus*) with some Scottish rush (*Juncus trifidus*), which is locally common on rock ledges and the stony parts of the moorlands, heath rush (*Juncus squarrosus*), cottongrass (*Eriphorum angustifolium*), cowberry (*Vaccinium Vitis-idaea*) and bilberry (*Vaccinium myrtillus*), which in Scotland is called blaeberry. This plant is often dominant on the higher ground and under tree cover where the heather thins out.

The wettest areas of moorlands are the bogs, their main constituents being the mosses *Sphagnum papillosum*, and *S. rubellum*, the insectivorous sundews (*Drosera rotundifolia*), the great sundew (*Drosera anglican*), and bog asphodel (*Narthecium ossifragum*). The pools may contain bogbean (*Menyanthes trifoliata*). The insect larvae, seeds and small invertebrates form the main source of food for the smaller birds and the birds of prey find a plentiful supply during the breeding season of small birds, mammals, amphibians and eggs. Many of the birds which nest in the moorlands migrate for the winter months, some as far as the Mediterranean and Africa. However, the red grouse remains in Scotland.

A moorland scene near Dolgellau showing the photographer's hide, in the foreground. Inset above: Hen Harrier in flight and below: the Meadow Pipit photographed from the hide.

Left and below: male Buzzard and chicks
Above: male Snow Bunting
Below right: Carrion Crow

SNOW BUNTING

Plectrophenax nivalis

These buntings are mainly winter visitors, although occasionally they do nest on the high tops of Scottish mountains. They are inconspicuous on the ground, although attractively coloured when in flight, and their white patches are clearly visible. They are gregarious and in winter large flocks are often observed, on sand-dunes and shingle beaches as well as mountains and rough grasslands. In the summer the black and white plumage of the males is distinctive; the females have brown back feathers. They measure in length 16.5cm. Their food includes seeds, insects, beetles and some grain. Their nests are made of mosses and dried vegetation and lined with hair, and are usually located on mountain screes and well hidden. They have a whistling 'tweet' call.

BUZZARD

Buteo buteo

They are the most common of the large birds of prey in Britain and are found mainly in western and northern parts. Persecution caused their disappearance from Ireland until about twenty years ago, when they started to breed again. Rabbits formed an important part of their food and when myxomatosis occurred in 1954, and greatly reduced the rabbit population, buzzards had to find other sources of food such as rats, mice, voles and beetles. The sexes are similar in appearance, and measure in length 50–59cm. They nest in trees, on rough ground, on rock ledges, and the nest resembles a large bundle of sticks. During their soaring flights with their broad wings flapping lazily and their wing-tips widely stretched, they frequently call, with a sound similar to the mewing of a cat.

CARRION CROW

Corvus corone corone

Crows as a family are considered to be the most intelligent of birds. Carrion crows are widespread throughout England and Wales and in southern Scotland, where they overlap with the hooded crow, their northern counterpart, with which they inter-breed. They do not assemble in such large gatherings as rooks, but they do gather in families during summer and they become more gregarious during winter. The sexes are similar in appearance and they measure in length 47cm. Their nests are located mainly in trees and sometimes on cliff ledges, and are made of twigs and dried vegetation, sometimes being lined with wool and feathers. In addition to young birds and eggs, their food includes small mammals, insects and their larvae, fruit, grain and carrion. They have a repeated raucous 'kraaa' call.

HOODED CROW

Corvus corone cornix

These counterparts of the carrion crows are widespread in north-eastern Scotland and Ireland. Often they are called 'hoodies'. Their presence is not appreciated by gamekeepers, as they do eat the eggs and nestlings of grouse. The sexes are similar in appearance and they measure in length 47cm. Their nests are usually located in trees or heather and they are made with twigs and heather and lined with wool. In addition to eggs and nestlings, their food includes carrion, insects, fruit and some vegetable matter. Their call is the same as the carrion crow – a repeated 'kraaa'.

Hooded Crow at nest lined with sheep's wool.

CURLEW

Numenius arquata

These large waders are common throughout the British Isles and easily recognised by their long curved bills and their distinctive call 'cur-li'. During the spring and summer they are found on moorlands, marshes, bogs and meadows and during the winter they appear in large flocks on mud-flats and salt-marshes. The sexes are similar in appearance. They measure in length 56cm. They nest in hollows in grass or heather and the nest itself is made of grasses, sedges, and lined with heather. Their food consists of molluscs, small fish and crustacea during the winter and insects, berries, seeds and earthworms in summer.

DIPPER

Cinclus cinclus

These birds are adapted to an aquatic life and are often seen on rocks in fast-running rivers and streams bobbing up and down as though in rhythm with moving water. They will also walk along the bottoms of rivers in the search for food, and they are good swimmers. Their white throats and breast patches are very distinctive, both sexes being similar in appearance; they measure in length 18cm. Their diet consists of small fish, caddis-flies and larvae, tadpoles and earthworms. Their nests are located in banks and under bridges above flowing water, and are made of mosses, grass, dried leaves and bracken. Their call note is a 'zit-zit'.

RED-THROATED DIVER

Gavia stellata

They are about the same size as the black-throated diver and smaller than the great northern diver. Their most significant identifying feature, apart from the red throat, is their uptilted bills. The plumage of the sexes is similar, and they measure in length 56cm. Their nests are close to water and the eggs are laid on flattened rushes or grass tussocks. Food consists mainly of fish, molluscs and amphibians. Their voice is a guttural 'kwack'.

Left: Red-throated Diver makes an alarm call

DOTTEREL

Eudromias morinellus

These very tame birds are confined to the Cairngorms and neighbouring mountains. They are very rare passage migrants in Ireland. The male birds are responsible for the incubation of the eggs. Their nests are located on the high plateaux of mountains and are scrapes in the ground, and lined with lichens or mosses. The females are slightly larger and their plumage is brighter than that of the males. They measure in length 21–23cm. Their diet consists of insects, spiders and some berries. They have a whistling call.

DUNLIN

Calidris alpina

These small shore birds are easily identifiable in summer because of their black bellies. During the winter their slightly down-curved bills help to distinguish them from the other small waders probing for animal life in the tidal mud. Their nests are usually located on moorlands, bogs and salt-marshes, and are to be found in tussocks, lined with dried grasses and leaves. The sexes are similar in appearance; they measure in length 18cm. Their food consists of molluscs, crustacea, worms, insects and larvae.

Above: a female Dotterel about to take off
Right: Dunlin in winter plumage

GOLDEN EAGLE

Aquila chrysaetos

These majestic birds with their seven-foot wingspan are a magnificent spectacle as they soar high in the hills in their search for prey. When diving towards their prey they often reach speeds of 155kph. The male is slightly smaller than the female; they measure in length respectively 79cm and 86cm. They nest mainly on rock ledges, but sometimes in trees. The nest is large and untidy, consists of sticks, heather, and bracken, and is lined with dried rushes. Their diet consists of ptarmigan, red grouse, hares, rabbits, voles, mice and carrion. Occasionally, they will eat deer calves and lambs. Their calls are often described as yaps and yells.

GREENSHANK

Tringa nebularia

These sleek birds are more easily observed during the non-breeding seasons, when they frequent estuaries and marshes in search of food, which consists of small fish, molluscs, crustacea, insects and larvae. They measure in length 30cm. Their nests are very difficult to locate; usually they are not far from water and are a scrape in the ground among stones, heather or mosses, lined with dried vegetation. They are migratory. Their song is a 'too-ho' which is repeated.

RED GROUSE

Lagopus lagopus

These grouse have been regarded as unique to the British Isles, but are now considered to be close relatives of the Scandinavian willow grouse. They are mainly birds of the upland areas, where heather or ling (*Calluna vulgaris*) dominate, together with some bilberry and crowberry. The fresh shoots, flowers and berries form the main source of their food. In Ireland, although favouring heather-moors, they are also found on lowland bogs. Their nests are scrapes or depressions in the ground and lined with dried vegetation. The females have paler colouring and are slightly smaller than the male birds; the males measure in length 38cm and the females 35cm. They have a cackling 'kok-kok' call.

Above: Greenshank
Right: Red Grouse

BLACK-HEADED GULL

Larus ridibundus

These gulls are mis-named, as the head is not black, but a dark brown. Colonies of these birds are scattered throughout the British Isles. In winter, however, the dark head is reduced to a dark stripe behind the eye. They measure in length 35cm. They are very noisy not only during the breeding season, but also during the winter when competing for food with other members of their colony. Some birds migrate after the breeding season. Diet consists of almost anything that is available, including kitchen scraps and offal in towns and, elsewhere, insects, earthworms, leather-jackets, crustacea and eggs and young of a variety of birds. They nest in colonies; some are very large, numbering many thousands of birds. The nest is made from dried vegetation on tussocks and sometimes on bare ground. They have many calls – one frequently heard is a raucous 'kwaar'.

Above: an adult Gull clearly shows the black head
Below: an adult in winter without its black head markings

65

COMMON GULL

Larus canus

The word common is not descriptive of these birds, although they are not rare; both herring gulls and black-headed gulls have much greater populations. Although common gulls range widely during winter, during the breeding season they are confined to moorlands, islands, shingle beaches, bogs and marshes. The nests are located on the ground and usually in small colonies. They are scavengers and their diet is very varied, as apart from kitchen refuse they eat molluscs, crustacea, small fish, insects, earthworms, seeds and also eggs and young birds. They are similar in appearance to the herring gull, but smaller; they measure in length 40cm. Their call is a 'kik-kik-kik' and sometimes a whistling 'keeya'.

HEN HARRIER

Circus cyaneus

They are characteristic birds of the open country where they can be seen flying low over the ground in their search for small mammals. The numbers of these birds has increased and this could be due to the increase of young conifer plantations and the protection now given to hawks. Male birds are quite different from females, with blue-grey feathers contrasting with those of the females which are brown. The female is larger than the male; they measure in length respectively 49cm and 43cm. In addition to small mammals they eat birds and invertebrates. Their nests are on the ground and are usually pads of aquatic vegetation with heather and bracken and lined with dried grasses. They have a feeble call.

MERLIN

Falco columbarius

These very small and courageous birds are usually observed flying low and swiftly over open moorland in search of food, which consists mainly of small birds such as meadow pipits, wheatears, finches, buntings, ring ouzels, dunlin and other waders. Some insects also are eaten. The males, during the breeding season, will transfer their catch to the female in flight. The males are slightly smaller than the females, measuring 28cm, while the latter are up to 30cm in length. Males have blue-grey feathers on their backs and the females have a brown head and a brown back with whitish speckles on their tail feathers. Their nests are located on the ground and usually hidden by heather or other vegetation. Occasionally, they will use other birds' abandoned nests. The males' call is a quick series of short notes 'ke-ke-ke'.

RING OUZEL

Turdus torquatus

Although very similar to the familiar blackbird, they are identified easily, because of the distinctive white crescents on their breasts and their preference for mountain and moorland habitats throughout the British Isles.

Far left above: Common Gull
Far left below: female Hen Harrier
Above left: a young Merlin threatens the photographer
Below left: male Hen Harrier

67

SHORT-EARED OWL

Asio flammeus

As their name implies their 'ear-tufts' are very short. They are usually seen flying low over moorland during daylight in their search for voles. When in flight their wings are tilted upwards and so they can be mistaken for harriers, who hunt over similar ground. Their nests are located on the ground in tussocks of grass, heather or rushes. The sexes are similar in appearance and they measure about 38cm. In addition to voles, their diet consists of mice, small birds and insects. Although usually silent, they do make a barking call when their nesting site is threatened.

SNOWY OWL

Nyctea scandiaca

These attractive owls returned to the Shetland Isles to breed in 1967, where the terrain of open grassland and heather-moor with rocky outcrops approximates to their Scandinavian habitats. They are also winter and summer visitors to the moorlands and marshes of mainland Scotland, the Orkneys and the Hebrides. They do not construct a nest, but lay their eggs in depressions in the ground. Both sexes have almost pure-white plumage and they measure in length 61 cm. Their food includes small mammals, small birds and also some fish. They are usually silent birds, but do occasionally utter a loud shriek.

Above: Short-eared Owl, two and a half weeks old
Right: Snowy Owl

MEADOW PIPIT

Anthus pratensis

These common birds of moorlands, grasslands and meadows migrate to France and the Iberian peninsula in the autumn and return in the spring. The sexes are similar in appearance and they measure in length about 14.5cm. Their nests are located in tussocks, ditches and grassy banks and are made of dried vegetation and lined with hair. Their call is a rapid and sometimes repeated 'tweep'.

GOLDEN PLOVER

Pluvialis apricaria

The most characteristic sign of the presence of these moorland birds is their sorrowful alarm call 'teee' – their gold and black upper parts blend so well with the vegetation as to make them inconspicuous. The sexes are similar in appearance and they measure in length about 28cm. They breed on low and high moorlands and the nests are neat cups of grasses, lined with mosses and lichens. Their diet consists of insects, snails, earthworms and small shellfish, some seeds and berries.

PTARMIGAN

Lagopus mutus

These birds of the grouse family are birds of the high mountains, seldom seen below 350m. They are extremely tame and are preyed upon by golden eagles and foxes. Their white winter plumage sometimes remains until the breeding season commences. The summer plumage of both sexes varies from light to dark shades with spots and bars. Their nests are scrapes in the ground, sometimes lined with dried vegetation and often placed near rock debris and sheltered by rock overhangs. Their diet consists of bilberries, crowberries, shoots, seeds and occasional insects. The females lack the males' black eye marking. They measure in length 28cm.

Below: a pair of Ptarmigan and right: winter plumage

RAVEN

Corvus corax

These large members of the crow family are frequently seen flying in pairs high above the remote parts of the countryside. Of course, the most famous of all ravens are those at the Tower of London. Much folklore is associated with ravens and it is foretold that if the ravens leave the Tower then disaster will befall the country. The sexes are similar in appearance and they measure in length 63.5cm. Their diet consists mainly of carrion, some small birds and mammals, and they will attack lambs. Their nesting sites are on cliff ledges, in the tops of trees and occasionally on deserted buildings. The nest is a massive collection of twigs and lined with hair, wool and dried vegetation. Their call is a deep throated croak.

REDSHANK

Tringa totanus

These red-legged birds are usually observed with other waders on the mud-flats as they probe for food, but during the breeding season they seek a more solitary life, concealing their nests among the tussocks of grass and rushes on moorland and marshy lowland pastures. The sexes are similar in appearance; they measure in length 28cm. Their food includes molluscs, crustacea, worms, insects and some vegetable matter. A distinctive characteristic of these birds is their loud alarm call 'teuk-teuk'.

COMMON SANDPIPER

Tringa hypoleucos

These small waders visit our shores in spring for their breeding grounds close to the lakes of north-west England and the lochs of Scotland; they are well distributed along the shores of the loughs, rivers and streams in Ireland. Their nests are scrapes or depressions in the ground, lined with grasses and are usually well concealed. Their food includes insects, small molluscs, snails, tadpoles and some vegetable matter. The sexes are similar in appearance; they measure in length 21cm. They have a liquid 'twee-wee-wee' call.

Below left: Raven. This bird is a Tower raven and below: Redshank

TWITE

Acanthis flavirostris

The most distinctive features of these birds are the pinkish plumage of the males' rump and, in winter, the yellow bills of both sexes. The females are light brown with dark streaks. In the winter they desert the mountains and moorlands for more southerly rough pastures.

WHEATEAR

Oenanthe oenanthe

These spring arrivals from Africa are commonly seen flying to their moorland and grassland haunts, their distinctive white rumps clearly visible. The males have blue-grey backs, this colouring being less prominent during the winter. The females throughout the year have a brown plumage. They measure in length 14–15cm. They nest in holes in the ground, under boulders and sometimes in old rabbit burrows. The nests are made of dried grasses and lined with wool and hair. Their food includes insects, their larvae, spiders, beetles and snails. They have a harsh 'chuck-weet' call.

BIRDS OF THE RIVERS, LAKES AND MARSHES

Freshwater habitats are probably the most rewarding for bird-watchers, especially during the winter months when our resident birds are joined by visitors who come south to avoid the harsher conditions of their breeding grounds in northern Europe. Two birds which greatly enhance the British winter scene are the Bewick's and whooper swans. They can be distinguished from our resident mute swan which, when swimming, holds its neck in a graceful curved position whereas the Bewick's and whooper swans hold their necks in a stiffly erect position.

On the credit side some of man's activities have been beneficial to birds who favour freshwater habitats by creating areas such as the Norfolk Broads, reservoirs, gravel pits and sewage farms. Not only has this activity helped to increase populations, but has also contributed to the spread of many species throughout these islands.

On the debit side man is responsible for the pollution of many freshwater habitats by releasing effluent directly into rivers. There has recently been an improvement in the treatment of sewage and the disposal of industrial waste, and so some amelioration of freshwater habitats has been achieved. The Norfolk Broads, with its shallow water and earth banks, is suffering because the wash of the numerous boats during the holiday periods is causing the banks to collapse, and the propellers of the motorboats are cutting the weeds on which many of the birds feed.

Mute swans are the victims of Britain's most popular outdoor sport, fishing. Over 3,000,000 anglers participate in this activity annually. The swans die from lead poisoning after swallowing the lead pellets which have become detached from the angler's fishing line or gut. Many fish-eating birds are killed by eating fish which themselves have eaten insects that have been killed by synthetic insecticides. Nitrates and phosphates are two of the most important fertilisers that are being washed off the land by rain into marshes, rivers and streams. In large enough quantities, they will cause the loss of oxygen in the water, and so kill both plant and animal life.

During and since the Second World War it has been the

The river Kennet near Newbury with inset above: Marsh Harrier in flight and below: Coots fighting practice of many farmers to fill in small ponds to increase the land area for cultivation. This practice has reduced considerably the habitats of moorhens, coots and ducks. The pollution and destruction of the small and numerous freshwater habitats occurs almost imperceptibly, and hence it is difficult to assess the seriousness of its threat to the future of plants and birds.

AVOCET

Recurvirostra avosetta

Some 200 years ago the avocets were plentiful but, due to drainage and exploitation by man, they eventually disappeared from the British Isles. In 1947, these attractive wading birds became re-established on our shores at Havergate Island which subsequently became a National Nature Reserve. Their breeding site has been protected by the Royal Society for the Protection of Birds and this protection has been most successful; the breeding pairs have increased, although a number of set-backs were experienced, caused by rat predation of the eggs and flooding. They migrate southwards during the winter. The sexes are similar in appearance; they measure in length 43cm. Their nests are located among salt-marsh vegetation or simply hollows in sand, but always near shallow water or brackish lagoons. They have a musical 'kloot' call.

BITTERN

Botaurus stellaris

These birds of the reed-beds are often heard but seldom seen. Their 'booming' call is unique among birds. They have mottled brown plumage which merges perfectly with the reeds.

Below: Avocet; above right: Reed Bunting and below right: Coots nesting

REED BUNTING

Emberiza schoeniclus

They are widespread throughout the British Isles and the resident population is augmented by winter visitors from northern Europe. They are found on pasture land with ditches, marshlands and reed-beds. The males' heads are black, a feature less obvious on the females, whose heads are much duller. They measure in length 15cm. Their nests are on or near the ground and are constructed of grasses, rushes and lined with hair. Occasionally their nests are exploited by cuckoos. Their food includes seed, insects and their larvae, and small molluscs. They have a deep 'churr' call.

COOT

Fulica atra

These water-birds are widely distributed throughout the lakes, reservoirs and water-filled gravel pits of the British Isles. The sexes are similar in appearance, measuring in length 38 cm. Their substantial nests, found on the margins of lakes and ponds and sometimes on floating platforms, are made of reeds and other aquatic vegetation. They feed mainly on vegetable matter with some fish, newts, tadpoles and other birds' eggs. Their call is a loud explosive 'kowt'.

75

BLACK-THROATED DIVER

Gavia arctica

They are smaller than the great northern divers and their black throats and white stripes on the sides of their necks and breasts distinguish them from the red-throated divers. They are not very common and mainly occur in Scotland.

TUFTED DUCK

Aythya fuligula

These very popular diving ducks are common on lakes and ponds throughout the British Isles. The resident bird population is augmented by visitors from Scandinavia and Iceland. The drake has a long crest, while the duck's crest is shorter and her plumage is brown. They measure in length 43cm. Their nests are found on the ground in grasses or rushes close to water and they are made of grasses and lined with down. Their food includes water plants, insects and small fish.

GADWALL

Anas strepera

Among the rarest of the British breeding ducks, these have a preference for lakes, lochs and marshy ponds. The plumage of the ducks is duller than that of the drakes and they measure in length 51 cm. They usually nest in dense vegetation close to water. The nest is found on the ground and is made with grasses, reeds and other vegetation mixed with down. Their food includes vegetable matter with some worms and molluscs. The call of the drake is a 'whek-whek' croaking note.

Below: Tufted Duck drake: above right: Gadwall duck and right: Garganey drake

GARGANEY

Anas querquedula

These ducks migrate from Africa to their principal breeding grounds in Scandinavia, but a small number stop in the British Isles to breed. Their nesting sites are usually on marshes, and sometimes on wet meadows and fenlands. The nest is made of grasses and down. The handsome drake contrasts with the female whose plumage is a mottled brown. They measure in length 38 cm. The male has a deep cackling note and the female a mallard-like 'quack'. Their food includes molluscs, insects, worms, beetles and vegetable matter including leaves, roots and seeds.

BLACK-TAILED GODWIT

Limosa limosa

Although these attractive birds are mainly passage migrants and winter visitors, very occasionally they breed in the marshes and wet meadows of East Anglia. The sexes are similar in appearance; they measure in length 41cm. Their nests are well hidden scrapes or hollows in the ground amongst grass or scrubby vegetation and lined with grasses and leaves. Their food includes beetles, grasshoppers, mayflies, snails and earthworms. Their call is a loud 'weeka-weeka-weeka'.

Male Goldeneye

GOLDENEYE

Bucephala clangula

Goldeneyes are mainly winter visitors and passage migrants to the British Isles. Usually they are seen around the coast and estuaries as well as on inland waters. The drake's black and white colouring contrasts greatly with that of the brown and grey duck. They measure in length 46 cm. Only two instances of breeding in the British Isles have been recorded. Their food includes chiefly molluscs, insects, earthworms and tadpoles. They are mainly silent birds, though the drake has a harsh grating call.

78

GOOSANDER

Mergus merganser

Similar to mergansers and smews (also known as 'saw-bills'), goosanders' breeding grounds are usually lakes and rivers where trees are present. During the winter months they frequent rivers, lakes and reservoirs. Their nests are mainly found in holes in trees, but when trees are absent they will nest in peat banks and rock crevices. Very little nest material is used apart from some grasses and heather, with accumulated down for lining. The drake's dark green head and neck contrasts with the female's chestnut-coloured head. Their food consists almost entirely of fish and this preference has been the cause of their persecution. The male's display call is a croaking 'karr'. They measure in length 66 cm.

CANADA GOOSE

Branta canadensis

These geese were introduced from Canada to parks in the 18th century. Many birds escaped and wild colonies became established in England and there are scattered colonies in Scotland, northern Ireland and Wales. Their 'honking' flight call is becoming very familiar as their numbers and range increase. The sexes are similar in appearance; they measure in length 95cm. They are very effective 'lawn mowers', as they crop the grass very close to the ground. In addition to grasses, their food includes cereals and some insects. Their nests are depressions in the ground, and lined with vegetation and feathers.

Canada Geese

BLACK-NECKED GREBE

Podiceps nigricollis

They are easily identified by their black faces and necks and golden coloured tufts behind their eyes. In the winter the tufts are not visible. They winter on lakes and coastal waters. They breed very rarely in Scotland.

LITTLE GREBE OR DABCHICK

Tachybaptus ruficollis

These are the smallest of the British grebes and are widespread on ponds, lakes and slow-flowing rivers. They are distinguishable from other grebes by their lack of head adornments at all seasons. Their nests are large mounds of water-weeds attached to reeds, rushes and other marginal vegetation. Their food includes small fish, molluscs, insects and some vegetable matter. The female's colouring is duller than that of the male and they measure in length 23 cm. They have a whistling 'whit-whit' call.

Above right: Dabchick
Right: a pair of Great-crested Grebes at their nest

80

GREAT CRESTED GREBE

Podiceps cristatus

All grebes are aquatic diving birds. The great crested grebes are the largest of those seen on our lakes, reservoirs, large ponds and flooded gravel pits. Their ear-tufts, which resemble a pair of horns, are most distinctive. Their courtship displays are spectacular, especially when both birds emerge after diving and 'stand' on the water breast to breast with their necks erect. The sexes are similar in appearance and measure in length 48 cm. Their nest consists of a pile of weeds which, when floating, is attached to growing vegetation. Their food includes freshwater fish, insects and larvae, newts and tadpoles and vegetable matter. Their call is a loud barking 'kar-a-ah' or 'gorrr'.

MARSH HARRIER

Circus aeruginosus

These birds, very rare in these islands, are confined almost entirely to eastern England, where they hunt over the reed-beds and marshes. The males are not as colourful as those of other harriers. They have blue-grey tails and wing feathers and the females are dark brown with a yellowish crown. The females are the larger, measuring in length 56cm, while the males measure 50cm. Their nests are made of dried vegetation and are located on the ground in marshy areas. Their food includes water-voles, birds, amphibians, reptiles and some carrion. The female's call is a high-pitched whistling and the male's call is a shrill 'kweao'.

Below: an adult Great-crested Grebe with a juvenile

This Heron chick is stimulating the parent bird to regurgitate food by rubbing its bill

HERON

Ardea cinerea

These very large birds are found throughout the British Isles and are common by lakes, rivers, streams and sometimes reservoirs, where they stand motionless like statues in the shallows waiting patiently for their prey. Their nests are usually built in colonies on the tops of trees and are made of sticks with some dried vegetation. The sexes are similar in appearance; they measure in length 90cm. Their food includes, fish, amphibians, water-voles, beetles and some nestlings. Their call is a harsh 'ka-ark'.

KINGFISHER

Alcedo atthis

These brilliantly coloured birds are found throughout England, Wales, Ireland and southern Scotland, but they are rare in northern Scotland. Their numbers fluctuate considerably, and this may be due to variations in the degree of severity of our winters. They are well adapted to the method they use for catching fish, diving headlong from a perch into the water with explosive speed to swoop upon the unsuspecting prey. The sexes are similar in appearance and they measure in length 16.5cm. Their nests are located at the ends of tunnels which they excavate in the banks of rivers, streams and lakes. In addition to fish, their diet includes water-beetles and tadpoles. Their call is a loud 'chee'.

MALLARD

Anser platyrhynchos

They are the most common of the British wild ducks, often seen on ponds and lakes in towns and cities. The drakes' attractive colouring is in contrast to the ducks' rather drab brown plumage. They measure in length 58cm. Their food includes water plants, seeds and large quantities of bread. Their nests are usually found in rough grass and sedges and are well hidden; they are made of grasses and lined with down from the duck's breast.

SAND MARTIN

Riparia riparia

These summer visitors from Africa range throughout the British Isles and they have a definite preference for open country with rivers, streams and ponds. They are gregarious birds and their nesting colonies, which are usually in the sandy banks of streams, rivers or sand pits, are often filled with shrill chatterings as the birds come and go to their nest-holes. The sexes are similar in appearance and they measure in length 12cm. Their food includes gnats, flies, beetles and other insects. They have a 'chirriping' call.

RED-BREASTED MERGANSER

Mergus serrator

During the breeding season they frequent freshwater lochs, rivers and islands on sheltered sea-lochs, especially in those areas with a plentiful cover of trees. In the winter months they are mainly to be seen in bays and estuaries and sometimes on lakes close to the coast. The drakes can be identified by their dark green heads and double crest, the ducks having a greyish-brown plumage. Their nests are well hidden in hollows in the ground and are lined with leaves and down. They measure in length 58 cm. Their food is chiefly fish with some worms and insects. The drakes are usually silent, but the female has a 'karr-r' call.

Below: Moorhen and right: female Red-breasted Merganser

MOORHEN

Gallinula chloropus

These familiar water-birds frequent a wide range of freshwater habitats including canals, small ponds and slow-flowing streams and rivers. The sexes are similar in appearance and measure in length 33 cm. Their nests, usually found in aquatic vegetation on the water's edge or attached to branches overhanging water, and sometimes in bushes near water, are made of dead water-plants. Their food consists mainly of vegetable matter and some insects and molluscs. They have a high-pitched alarm call 'kik-kik-kik'.

OSPREY

Pandion haliaetus

The fact that these spectacular fishing birds are breeding again in Scotland is largely due to the successful conservation project mounted by the Royal Society for the Protection of Birds. When two birds returned to Scotland after many years' absence, their nest was guarded to ensure successful incubation of the eggs. Subsequently, there has been slow but steady increase in the numbers of breeding birds. Their nests are always located near water; they are made from sticks and are mainly in trees, but sometimes occur on the ground. The sexes are similar in appearance and they measure in length 55cm. They live almost entirely on a fish diet. They have a whistling call.

RED-NECKED PHALAROPE

Phalaropus lobatus

An unusual feature of these birds is that the females' colouring is bolder than that of the males. The orange-red patches on their necks and their white throats are most distinctive. They swim rapidly in tight circles to disturb insects for food.

Above: an Osprey returns to its treetop eyrie with a salmon

PINTAIL

Anas acuta

Pintails are mainly winter visitors and passage migrants, although as a breeding species in the British Isles there is a slight increase. The male's long pointed tail makes identification easy, the female's tail, which is also pointed, being shorter. They measure in length 56 cm. Their nests are hollows in the ground, lined with grasses, leaves and down. Their food includes aquatic plants, insects, molluscs and worms. The male has a 'quuk-quuk' display note and the female a quacking note.

Above: female Pintail and centre: male Pintail
Below left: Little Ringed Plover

LITTLE RINGED PLOVER

Charadrius dubius

These small plovers have established themselves in eastern England and their range has spread since the 1930s. They favour freshwater localities, shingle beds, and sand and gravel pits, where they lay their eggs in hollows or scrapes in the ground. The sexes are similar in appearance; they measure in length 15cm. Their food includes insects, small molluscs and worms. Their call is a hissing 'tee-oo'.

POCHARD

Aythya ferina

These attractive small diving ducks enhance many of the lakes in our urban parks during autumn and winter. Unfortunately only a few birds remain in the British Isles to breed in the south-east of England. The drake's chestnut-red head contrasts with the brown head of the duck. They measure in length 45 cm. Their nests are usually found on ponds and lakes, where reeds provide cover. The nest consists of a large pile of reeds. Their food includes mainly vegetable matter and some crustacea and insects. They have a 'karr-rr' call.

Right and below: Pochards
Far right above: female Ruff
Far right below: Green Sandpiper

WATER RAIL

Rallus aquaticus

These birds are very shy and are more often heard than seen. They have a hard penetrating call. They are brown above, with slate-grey throat, breast and underparts. Their long red bills distinguish them from other water birds.

RUFF

Philomachus pugnax

In the past these birds bred commonly on our once extensive marshes which, over the years, have been greatly reduced by draining policies. Now they are passage migrants in spring and autumn. The bird's name is derived from the male's elaborate ruff which it displays when attracting a female. The female is called a reeve. The male birds are larger than the female, measuring in length 28 cm to the female's 23 cm. Their food includes insects, worms, molluscs and some seed. They are usually silent birds, but occasionally utter a 'too-whit' call.

GREEN SANDPIPER

Tringa ochropus

These solitary birds are winter visitors from northern Europe or passage migrants during spring and autumn. They have a preference for marshes, bogs, lakes and streams. A small number may remain in the south of England during the summer. The sexes are similar in appearance; they measure in length 23cm. Their food includes insects, snails, molluscs, worms, and vegetable matter. Their call is a shrill 'weet-weet-weet-weet'.

SMEW

Mergus albellus

These ducks are rare winter visitors to the British Isles and are seen mainly on lakes, reservoirs, ponds and sometimes estuaries. They have serrated edges to their bills and are often referred to as 'saw-bills'. The drake's plumage is most attractive and is mainly white with a black eye patch, the female's colouring being greyer with a much darker head. The drake measures in length 48 cm and the female 43 cm. Their food consists mainly of fish and sometimes a little vegetable matter. They are silent birds, although occasionally the females utter a 'karr-r' note.

SHOVELER

Anas clypeata

These ducks get their name from their heavy bills, which are ideally adapted for feeding on the surfaces of lochs, lakes and ponds. They breed mainly in meadows close to water, but sometimes on commons and heaths. Their nests are usually hollows in the ground under grass or rushes, and are made with grasses, heather and dead reeds and lined with down and feathers. The colourful plumage of the drakes contrasts with the mottled brown colouring of the ducks. They measure in length 51 cm. Their food includes molluscs, insects and aquatic plants. The drake has a 'took-took' display call.

Above: female Smew and left: male Smew

SNIPE

Gallinago gallinago

These birds of the marshes, bogs and wet meadows are widespread in such habitats throughout the British Isles. Their numbers are augmented by visitors from northern Europe during the winter months. Outside the breeding season they are often observed in loose flocks. Their nests are located in rushes and tussocks of grass near fresh water. The sexes are similar in appearance; they measure in length 27cm. Their food is mainly worms, snails, water-beetles and some seeds. They have a grating 'scaap' call when alarmed.

JACK SNIPE

Lymnocryptes minimus

These winter visitors from Scandinavia and northern Russia are smaller than common snipe and the lack of white feathers on their tails assists in identification. They have a preference for water-meadows, marshes and bogs.

BEWICK'S SWAN

Cygnus columbianus

They are the smallest of the three wild swans and it is their smaller size, compared with the larger whooper swan, which helps with identification. Also, they have a shorter yellow-coloured wedge on their bills. They are winter visitors or passage migrants from the arctic tundra of northern Europe. They have a preference for swamps, lakes, reservoirs and rivers. Often they penetrate to southern England. The sexes are similar in appearance; they measure in length 120cm. Their food consists mainly of water-plants. They have a 'honking' call in flight.

MUTE SWAN

Cygnus olor

They are easily distinguishable from the Bewick's and whooper swans by the deep orange colouring on their bills and, when swimming, by their gracefully curved necks. Both the whooper and the Bewick's swans hold their necks erect when swimming. Considerable concern is felt by conservationists regarding the increasing numbers of deaths of mute swans from lead poisoning and it is anticipated that legislation will be passed to protect these elegant birds from this unnecessary hazard. They are not as mute as their name suggests and will make a loud hissing noise if their nests are approached too closely. The males are called 'cobs' and the females 'pens'. The sexes are similar in appearance; they measure in length 150–160cm. Their nests are located on the ground and consist of large piles of sticks and vegetation. Their food consists almost entirely of water-plants, but includes amphibians and small fish.

Far left above: Bewick's Swan
Far left below: Mute Swan and cygnets
Above: Mute Swan
Left: Whooper Swan and young

WHOOPER SWAN

Cygnus cygnus

These winter visitors from northern Europe and the arctic regions of Asiatic Russia are fairly widespread in northern England, Scotland and Ireland. They are distinguished from the Bewick's swans by their larger size and the depth of the yellow colouring on their bills. They are found on both salt water and fresh water. Their food consists of water-plants and sometimes they graze the grass on the banks of rivers and lakes. The sexes are similar in appearance; they measure in length 150–160cm. Their call is similar to that of the Bewick's swan, a powerful 'honking'.

TEAL

Anas crecca

During the breeding season they have a preference for wet moorland, peat bogs and similar terrain. In the winter months they are found on lakes, reservoirs and ponds usually with an abundance of reeds. Often during the winter months they assemble in large numbers on estuaries. The drakes are most attractively coloured, but the females' plumage is mottled brown; both sexes have green and black patches on their wings. Their nests are made in hollows in the ground with grasses, leaves and bracken, and are lined with down and usually well concealed. They measure in length 35 cm. Their food includes chiefly aquatic vegetation and seeds and some insects and their larvae. The male has a 'krit-krit' call and the female a mallard-like 'quack'.

BLACK TERN

Chlidonias niger

These former breeding freshwater terns are now only passage migrants during spring and autumn. After wintering on the coasts and lakes of Africa they breed on the fens and meres of continental Europe. The sexes are similar in appearance and they measure in length 25 cm. Their food includes small fish, tadpoles and insects. They have a 'kik-kik' call.

Above left: male Teal and centre: female Teal
Below: Black Tern on nest with chick

REED WARBLER

Acrocephalus scirpaceus

These warblers are summer visitors and are confined mainly to England. The sexes are similar in appearance and they measure in length 13cm. Their nests are usually located in reed-beds and are well constructed deep cups of dried vegetation attached to the reed stems; they are frequently exploited by cuckoos. Their food includes insects and their larvae, and sometimes berries. Their call is a low powerful 'churr'.

SEDGE WARBLER

Acrocephalus schoenobaenus

These winter visitors from Africa range throughout the British Isles and have a preference for habitats containing reed-beds, marshes, water-meadows and hedgerows close to water. The sexes are similar in appearance and measure in length 13cm. Their nests are located in aquatic vegetation and bushes and are made of dried vegetation with a lining of hair, willow down and feathers. Their food includes gnats, water-beetles, damsel flies and caterpillars. Their call is a loud throaty 'tuc'.

YELLOW WAGTAIL

Motacilla flava

These summer visitors from Africa are found in a wide range of habitats for breeding and feeding. They are almost entirely confined to England and are only rarely observed in Scotland, Ireland and Wales. The females have slightly duller yellow colouring. They measure in length 16.5cm. Their nests are either depressions or scrapes in the ground and the nest material is dried vegetation with hair used for lining. Their food includes insects and their larvae, and beetles. Their call is a loud 'tseet'.

GREY WAGTAIL

Motacilla cinerea

These colourful wagtails range throughout the British Isles. They are commonly found near running water and are often associated with dippers. In the winter they move southwards to freshwater habitats and they have a liking for watercress beds. They select their nesting sites in cavities or ledges near running water and the nests are made of mosses and small twigs, and are lined with hair. During the breeding season the males have a black throat, and on the females these throat feathers are brown with some white flecks. They measure in length 20cm. Their food includes insects and their larvae and small molluscs. Their call is a sharp 'tissick'.

PIED WAGTAIL

Motacilla alba

They frequent the open countryside and agricultural land and are often to be found near ponds and streams. The black and white summer plumage of the males contrasts with the greyer plumage of the females. Their nests are located in a variety of sites including ledges on buildings, holes in walls, garages, garden sheds and sometimes earth banks. They are made of mosses, grasses, leaves and twigs with a lining of wool or hair. Pied wagtails have a distinctive undulating flight and their call is a 'tsch-zik'. Their food includes insects, beetles, flies and their larvae, and some seeds.

WIGEON

Anas penelope

Wigeon have a preference in the breeding season for Scottish lochs, rivers, and other freshwater areas on moorlands. During the winter months they are mainly maritime birds, assembling in large numbers. Their nests are located on the ground among bracken and heather, and are usually lined with down. The drake's colourful plumage contrasts with the duck's, which is rufous-brown. Their food includes mainly vegetable matter including eel-grass and other grasses. The male's call is a musical 'whee-oo'. They measure in length 46 cm.

BIRDS OF THE SEA-CLIFFS

The coastline of the British Isles, which measures about 7150 linear miles, contains some of the most spectacular scenery to be seen in Europe. These cliffs are made up from a wide variety of rock types, which include the granites of Cornwall, the beautiful carboniferous limestones of Pembrokeshire and the Great Orme of North Wales, the chalk cliffs of Beachy Head, Sussex, the cathedral-like basalt columns of Fingal's Cave, Staffa and the Giant's Causeway in Co Antrim, and the old red sandstone of the Island of Noss, Shetland Islands. These varying forms of sea-cliffs apart from their beauty contain a wide range of habitats for plants and birds. Although plants are sparse, many species may be represented. The rock ledges and crevices, which trap the humus and moisture to allow plant growth, also provide resting places and nesting platforms and holes for colonies of sea-cliff birds.

The density of most sea-birds nesting on sea-cliffs has increased and their distribution has spread. However, there is a growing threat to sea-birds because of pollution. The auks are very vulnerable to oil pollution; for example, after the *Torrey Canyon* disaster the majority of oiled birds were auks. Puffins have declined considerably over the last fifty years, due possibly to predation by gulls and self-destruction of their nesting holes. Fulmars are becoming the most numerous of the sea-cliff nesting birds, their numbers having increased from a few hundred pairs at the beginning of the century to over 350,000 pairs around the coasts of the British Isles.

Photography of birds on high precipitous cliffs is exhilarating and enjoyable, but there are dangers, especially where the rock is loose or there is a strong wind. So the photographer must be vigilant at all times and not only concerned with his own personal safety but also for the safety of his valuable equipment. It is advisable to work with a companion for security and reassurance, preferably a person with some climbing experience. At all times, moreover, concern for the birds' well-being must be paramount.

Near Land's End with inset above: Gannet in flight. These birds can have a wing span of 1.8 metres. Inset below: Fulmar

CHOUGH

Pyrrhocorax pyrrhocorax

These acrobatic birds are now rare along the coasts of the British Isles. Occasionally, they can be observed near the entrances of old mine-shafts in Snowdonia or on the west coast of Scotland. Choughs often gather in groups and they nest in caves, ruins and in crevices on sea-cliffs. Their nests are made with twigs and grasses and are lined with sheep's wool. The sexes are similar in appearance; they measure in length 38cm. Their food includes insects and their larvae, spiders, worms and some corn. Their calls include a yelping 'kyaa' or 'Chuff'.

CORMORANT

Phalacrocorax carbo

These large black birds, with their long necks and white patches below their eyes, are common residents along the coasts of the British Isles. Frequently, they can be observed on inland waters and tidal rivers. They are strongly 'colonial', building their nests close together, usually on ledges and shelves on the higher parts of cliff-faces and sea-stacks; inland they nest in trees. Their nests are made of sticks, seaweed, grasses and any other convenient material available. Their flight is similar to that of shags and is direct and low over the water. When seen at close quarters their black plumage has a bronze-like sheen. Their feathers are not water-proofed and, like the shags, they are often seen drying their feathers in the breeze. They are voracious fish-eaters, pursuing their prey under water from surface dives. The sexes are similar in appearance; they measure in length 100cm.

ROCK DOVE

Columba livia

These doves are the ancestors of the feral and domestic pigeons and are now only locally common in the British Isles. They are found mainly on the sea-cliffs of western Scotland and Ireland. Many of the habitats once occupied by rock doves are now used by feral pigeons. They nest in crevices and on ledges, often in caves, and their nests are made of twigs. The sexes are similar in appearance; they measure in length 38cm. Their food includes seeds, grain, vegetables and molluscs. Their 'cooing' call is similar to that of the feral pigeon.

Left: Cormorants and right: Rock Dove Below: female Peregrine Falcon and young. Peregrines mate for life.

PEREGRINE FALCON

Falco peregrinus

Unfortunately, these attractive falcons which were formerly quite common are now becoming rare, as they are the victims of pesticides. Either the birds themselves are poisoned, or their eggs are rendered infertile, because their favourite prey is pigeons and these may have eaten crops which have been sprayed. The toxic matter accumulates in the peregrines' bodies. They are considered to be the fastest flying birds, and speeds of 275kph during dives or stoops have been claimed for them. The males are called tiercels; the females are larger and they have distinctive brown-streaked underparts. They have a 'kek-kek-kek' call. They measure in length 43–45cm.

FULMAR

Fulmaris glacialis

These common birds of the open oceans come ashore only to breed. They are superficially gull-like, but their flight, gliding and banking on stiff narrow wings, is unmistakable. Another identifying feature is their tubular nostrils. The female lays one white egg on a bare rock ledge or scrape. They are more common in the north of England and Scotland, but their breeding range now extends to Norfolk and the chalk cliffs of Kent. When alarmed they are likely to eject a foul viscous green fluid with a musky odour at the intruder. The sexes are similar in appearance; they measure in length 47cm. Their food includes fish and crustacea.

GANNET

Sula bassana

The largest colony of gannets in the world is on the National Nature Reserve of St. Kilda, west of the Outer Hebrides. There is another famous colony on the Bass Rock, in the Firth of Forth. Most of the world's gannets are hatched on the sea-cliffs and stacks of the most remote parts of the British Isles. Their nests are made from seaweeds and grasses. The sight of gannets diving like arrows to catch fish is one of the most spectacular to be seen near sea-bird colonies. The sexes are similar in appearance; they measure in length 108cm.

BLACK GUILLEMOT

Cepphus grylle

These members of the auk family range along the rocky coasts of the British Isles and they are easily distinguished from the common guillemots by the white patches on their wings.

COMMON GUILLEMOT

Uria aalge

These small marine diving birds are numerous along the coastal waters of the British Isles. During the breeding season they occupy the precipitous sea-cliffs and tops of sea-stacks, where they incubate their eggs on bare rocks. The females lay one very large pear-shaped egg, the colours and markings of which are very variable – this may aid identification on a crowded ledge. The young descend to the sea after two weeks, where they continue to be fed by their parents. Their flight is swift and direct with rapid wing-beats. They catch fish by pursuing them under water, using their wings as well as their feet. The sexes are similar in appearance; they measure in length 42cm.

Far left above: Fulmars
Far left below: Gannet and chick
Left: Common Guillemots and below:
a colony on the Farne Islands

GREATER BLACK-BACKED GULL

Larus marinus

They are the largest of the British gulls and are formidable-looking when seen at close range. They have a more extensive distribution than their smaller relative, the lesser black-backed gull, extending westwards to Greenland and southwards to Spain and Portugal. The sexes are similar in appearance; they measure in length 75cm. Their food includes fish offal and carrion, and they will also take eggs and kill adult birds, especially puffins and shearwaters. Their nests are sometimes found on the ground, but more often on the tops of cliffs and stacks; they are made of seaweed, heather and grasses and any other convenient material.

LESSER BLACK-BACKED GULL

Larus fuscus

Apart from being smaller in size, they can be distinguished from their larger relatives, the greater black-backed gulls, by their yellow legs. Although they are mainly migratory birds, there is an increasing tendency to remain in the British Isles during winter, especially in urban areas and on refuse disposal dumps. They breed in colonies on vegetated tops or slopes of cliffs and their nests are made of twigs, seaweed and grasses. The sexes are similar in appearance; they measure in length 54cm.

Above: Greater Black-backed Gulls and juvenile
Right: Lesser Black-backed Gull

KITTIWAKE

Rissa tridactyla

These immaculate dove-like gulls are birds of the open seas. They come to land to breed in colonies on the rocky coasts of the British Isles; recently, however, they have started to breed on the softer chalk cliffs of Kent. Their nests are compact and neat structures with deep cups, composed mainly of grasses, seaweeds and mosses. They are built on narrow ledges, often at the entrance to caves. The sexes are similar in appearance; they measure in length 41cm. In addition to fish they eat insects and some molluscs. Their call, from which their name is derived, is a pleasant-sounding 'kitti-wake'.

The Kittiwake anchors its nest to the cliff with algae and guano; the young remain safely in the deep cup until they can fly

LEACH'S PETREL

Oceanodrama leucorrhoa

They are slightly larger than the storm petrels. Their colouring is mainly brown and they have forked tails. They breed in burrows on the remote islands of north and west Scotland.

STORM PETREL

Hydrobates pelagicus

These small oceanic birds have a dull black plumage, white rumps and squared black tails. They come ashore only to breed in island colonies off the western coasts of the British Isles. As well as excavating their own burrows for their nests, they also use old rabbit burrows.

ROCK PIPIT

Anthus spinoletta

These birds have adapted themselves to a life along the seashore, living mainly on the insects which inhabit the decaying seaweed. The sexes are similar in appearance; they measure in length 16.6cm. Their nests are usually located in rock crevices and are made of grasses and lined with hair. They have a 'tseep' call.

A typical group of Puffins photographed in Anglesey, North Wales

PUFFIN

Fratercula arctica

These rather comical-looking birds are sometimes called sea parrots. Unfortunately, their numbers are on the decline for reasons not yet understood. Their nests are usually on grass-covered sea-cliffs, where they excavate their burrows, or use old rabbit or shearwater holes for their nesting sites. They winter on the open sea; together with razorbills and guillemots they are the main victims of oil spills. The sexes are similar in appearance; they measure in length 32cm. Their food includes sand-eels, molluscs and small fish.

Puffins and below left: Rock Pipit

RAZORBILL

Alca torda

These birds are members of the auk family and are very efficient swimmers and divers. They spend most of the year on the open sea of the Atlantic Ocean, coming to the rocky cliffs only during the breeding season. They are gregarious and their single large eggs are usually located in crevices, under over-hangs, or sometimes on exposed ledges. Their food includes fish, sand-eels and worms. The sexes are similar in appearance; they measure in length 40cm.

SHAG

Phalacrocorax aristotelis

They are increasing in numbers and range and can be found breeding along the whole length of the coastline with the exception of east and south-east England. Unlike the cormorant they are very seldom seen away from the sea-cliffs and rocky shores but, like the cormorants, they are often seen with their wings outstretched drying their feathers after dives. The sexes are similar in appearance; they measure in length 85cm. Their nests are usually made of sticks and seaweed. Their diet is almost entirely of fish.

Above left and right: Razorbills, right: a Shag

MANX SHEARWATER

Puffinus puffinus

These birds fly prodigious distances after leaving their breeding sites in the summer; they journey to the south Atlantic, where they remain until returning to our rocky shores for the next breeding season. They have remarkable homing capabilities since, due to the danger of predation, they need to locate their nests during darkness. These are situated in burrows on turf-topped rocky islands, where the female lays a single white egg. At night, during courtship, they create a cacophony of shrieks and howls. Like all petrels they feed their young at night but these are then abandoned and have to live on their fat for some days before they can fly. The sexes are similar in appearance; they measure in length 35cm. Their food includes some molluscs, but mainly fish.

ARCTIC SKUA

Stercorarius parasiticus

These piratical birds merit this designation because of their habit of diving at gulls and terns, forcing them to disgorge their catch in mid-air, which the skuas then proceed to recover. Their breeding grounds are confined to northern Scotland and the Orkneys and Shetlands, where they nest among the grassy tussocks, a short distance away from the cliffs. The sexes are similar in appearance; they measure in length 66cm. In addition to disgorged fish they eat offal, eggs and some small birds.

Above: Shag on its nest

GREAT SKUA

Stercorarius skua

Like the arctic skua the great skua is a pirate, assailing other birds and robbing them of their catch. Locally they are called 'bonxies'. They are quite fearless and will attack, again and again, any human intruders who venture into their breeding areas. It can be a terrifying experience to see these large and ferocious-looking birds flying at your face, swerving upwards only inches away. They spend most of the year on the open sea, coming to land only during the breeding season. The sexes are similar in appearance; they measure in length 60cm. Their food, in addition to disgorged fish, includes offal and young birds.

BIRDS OF THE TOWNS, GARDENS AND PARKS

Those species that have availed themselves of these environments are the opportunists of the bird world. Their habitats have changed because of exploitation by man, and they have successfully adapted their lives to differing circumstances. These man-made habitats are most important for the conservation of birds for two reasons. First, they provide cover, nesting sites and food. Second, this close association with people produces a greater appreciation of their diversity, charm, beauty and needs and thus this intimate understanding will help to ensure the future not only of urban birds but of birds throughout the British Isles.

Two of the most familiar birds of the inner cities and towns are the feral pigeon and the house sparrow, who are almost entirely dependent upon the public for their food. Furthermore, factories, railway stations, office blocks, flats and houses are substitute nesting and roosting places for their former habitats on cliffs and rocky ledges. The feral pigeon is a descendant of the rock dove, although the present metropolitan population probably derived from escapes from dovecotes. Pigeons were bred in dovecotes to supplement man's diet, probably from about the Roman period onwards. The cheeky little house sparrow has been associated with human beings for many thousands of years and now is common in city centres, gardens, and, in particular, city parks where it finds a plentiful supply of partially eaten sandwiches and crumbs from under the tables of the outdoor cafes and restaurants.

The black redstart is a very good example of the opportunism shown by a bird whose habitat was formerly on sea-cliffs of southern England. During and after the Second World War this bird nested among the ruins of bombed sites in London. After the war it was a common sight to see Londoners watching these birds at Ludgate Hill, just below St. Paul's Cathedral. Since the 1950s many of these sites have been rebuilt and the black redstart has found alternative nesting sites on industrial buildings, quarries and sites of buildings being demolished for re-construction. A common sight at dusk in city centres is the invasion of the commuter starlings flying to their nightly roosts on ledges and roofs. These starlings are mainly resident. During the winter,

Inset above: Blue Tit. These little birds begin looking for nest sites early in the year so boxes should always be available by February.
Inset below: Spotted Flycatcher

111

however, there is an influx of northern European starlings which have a preference for trees in open country as perches for the night. Occasionally, their numbers are so great that the birds' sheer weight can break the branches of mature trees, and they also do damage to young plantations.

Recently, there has been a most dramatic spread of one particular bird in the British Isles. This is the collared dove, which has spread to these islands from the continent of Europe, where it is very common. The first collared doves bred here in 1955 and since then their breeding pairs can be numbered in the thousands. They have a preference for gardens, parks and farmyards.

The magpie is another bird which can be seen more often foraging for food in suburban gardens. In the past, persecution by gamekeepers could have been the reason for their wary behaviour towards man. They are guilty of taking eggs and the young of game and other birds. In northern Europe magpies are a very familiar sight in the towns where they roost on roofs and feed on scraps, instead of their more natural food of insects. Although more common in open spaces with trees and often near farm buildings, eventually they could become more numerous in towns and gardens.

The great tit, blue tit and the coal tit are familiar birds in suburban gardens, where they are frequent visitors to bird tables and feed on peanuts and coconuts hung out for them. Both the great tit and the blue tit have developed a successful technique for piercing the foil caps of milk bottles and partaking of the contents. A characteristic bird of the gardens and parks is the blackbird, which is probably the most numerous bird in the British Isles. It finds an ample supply of worms on lawns and suitable nesting sites in the shrubs and hedges of gardens and parks.

The robin, our national bird, is widely distributed throughout the British Isles. It is very friendly and seems to enjoy the company of humans, especially of gardeners when they are turning over the soil exposing grubs and centipedes. The affection and fascination the people of these islands hold for this tame little red-breasted bird is evidenced by the popularity of Christmas cards on which the robin appears and by the many poems celebrating its charms.

Right above: hen Blackbird feeding nestlings
Right centre: cock Blackbird
Right below: both Bullfinch parents at the nest

BLACKBIRD

Turdus merula

These ubiquitous birds with their delightful song and their chattering alarm call are familiar to us in our gardens and parks, which serve as a substitute for their former woodland habitat. They are probably the most numerous resident birds in the British Isles. The male is all black with a yellow bill and the female is dark brown with a brown bill. They measure in length 25cm. They will nest almost anywhere, but have a preference for hedgerows, bushes, trees and buildings. Their food consists of earthworms, insects, berries, seeds and household scraps.

BULLFINCH

Pyrrhula pyrrhula

These very handsome birds unfortunately are considered by many fruit growers as pests, because they eat the buds of trees, mainly in the winter, when other food such as seeds and berries is scarce. The female is less colourful than the male, even the black cap being duller. They measure in length 14.5cm. Their nests are formed of twigs and are usually found in dense cover. Their song consists of a soft 'teek-teek'.

CHAFFINCH

Fringilla coelebs

Probably the commonest finch in the British Isles. The male birds are more attractive than the female; although the white wing-bars are similar on both sexes, the pink breasts of the males contrast with the yellow-brown on the females. They measure in length 15cm. There has been a decline in their numbers and this is considered to be due to the destruction of hedgerows. They construct a most attractive nest of mosses and lichens, usually located in trees or hedgerows. Their food consists of seeds, insects and earthworms. They have a distinctive variable song consisting of 'chwink-chwink' terminating with a 'cheo-eeo'.

COLLARED DOVE

Streptopelia decaocto

These recent arrivals from the continent of Europe are now widespread throughout the countryside and their call 'coo-coo-coo' is a familiar sound, but one not always appreciated early in the mornings. They are mainly grain and seed-eaters, and consequently are often seen near barns and poultry-houses. The sexes are similar in appearance; they measure in length 28cm. They construct flat nests of twigs on ledges of buildings or in trees, especially of the cupressus family.

DUNNOCK

Prunella modularis

These birds are more commonly known as hedge sparrows, although they are unrelated to house and tree sparrows. The most distinctive feature is the bill which is finely tapered, whereas sparrows' bills are broader and adapted to seed eating. The sexes are similar in appearance; they measure in length 15cm. They are unobtrusive birds and, usually, are only seen for a fleeting moment as they move about in the bottoms of hedgerows in the search for insects. Their nests consists of twigs, wool, hair, mosses and feathers and are located usually in shrubs and brambles. Occasionally, they act as involuntary foster parents for cuckoos. Their song is a short high-pitched 'tseep'.

SPOTTED FLYCATCHER

Muscicapa striata

The word spotted is not descriptive of the adult birds, only the young having discernible spots. As their name implies, they are specialists in the art of catching flies. They are migratory and usually arrive rather late in the season, during May. The sexes are similar in appearance. They measure in length 14cm. Their nests are located in tree forks and on ledges, are made from wool, hair, mosses and lichens and are usually held together with spider's webs. Their song is a repetitive thin note.

Spotted Flycatchers return year after year to favourite sites

GOLDFINCH

Carduelis carduelis

These very attractive birds are now more numerous than at the beginning of the century, when they were trapped for sale as cage birds. The sexes are similar in appearance; they measure in length 12cm. They favour habitats where thistles and other seed bearing weeds grow. Their nests are made from roots, dried grass, mosses, and lichens, and are lined with plant down or wool. Their song is a flowing twitter, similar to canary song.

Above: Goldfinch
Right: Greenfinch

GREENFINCH

Carduelis chloris

These rather aggressive birds have adapted successfully to man-made habitats and are frequent visitors to bird-tables to feed on the peanuts placed in containers ostensibly for tits. The yellow wing-bars of the males are clearly seen when the bird is in flight, the females having a duller colouring. They measure in length 14cm. Their nests are made of grasses, wool, mosses and roots and are rather untidy. Their diet consists mainly of seeds, but with some fruit, berries and peanuts. They have a repeated 'chup' call.

HOUSE MARTIN

Delichon urbica

These birds are the most easily distinguished of the swallow family because of the distinctive white rump, which can be seen clearly when the birds are in flight. They measure in length 13cm. Their food is taken on the wing and only rarely do they alight on the ground, apart from the period when they collect mud for the construction of their nests. The under-parts of bridges and eaves are substitutes for their original nesting sites on cliffs and in caves. They have a chirruping call when in flight.

Nesting House Martin. As many as four hundred nests have been counted under one bridge near Shrewsbury

TAWNY OWL

Strix aluco

These owls are common in England, Wales and also most counties of Scotland apart from Sutherland, Caithness, and the Orkneys and Shetlands. They are absent from Ireland. They are nocturnal and favour areas near to human habitation – their shrill hooting call is frequently heard in gardens, parks and woodlands as it pierces the silence of the night. Both sexes are similar in appearance; they measure in length 38cm. They feed on small mammals, some birds, earthworms and insects. Their nests are located in tree holes, old buildings and occasionally on the ground.

Right: Tawny Owl and below: two owlets

FERAL PIGEON

Columba livia

These pigeons are the most visually obvious of all town-dwelling birds, especially in large city squares, where they take advantage of the centrally heated 'cliffs' and the abundance of food. In some areas they have reached pest proportions and the feeding of pigeons is prohibited. The sexes are similar in appearance, but their plumage can be very variable. They measure in length 33cm. Their nests are made with grass and twigs and they are very adaptable in their choice of sites, which includes ledges on buildings, balconies, walls and under the eaves of roofs. Apart from scrap food, their diet includes seeds and grain.

Male Black Redstart

BLACK REDSTART

Phoenicurus ochruros

Originally, these birds built their nests in sea-cliffs but, during the Second World War, they established themselves in the derelict and bombed sites of London. Since then many sites have been re-built and they have become adapted to a life on industrial sites, dockland, and in suburban London. The females' colouring is mainly brownish-grey, compared with the males' blackish-grey colouring during the winter. They measure in length 14cm. Their nests are found on ledges of buildings and walls and are of dried vegetation and mosses. Their food is mainly insects, spiders, seeds and berries.

119

ROBIN

Erithacus rubecula

These attractive and friendly birds are without doubt the most popular wild birds in Britain, although the tameness of the resident birds is not shown by the winter visitors from the Continent. These visitors are wary and very seldom approach human habitations, unless compelled to do so during severe winters when food is scarce, and they prefer the seclusion of woodlands. Although the resident robins are normally very peaceful, they can be very aggressive towards other robin intruders into their established territories. They select a wide variety of nesting sites, the most popular being holes in earth banks, walls and garden sheds, where they make their nests of mosses, grasses and hair, and line them with twigs. The juvenile robins are mottled and have brown tails. The sexes are similar in appearance; they measure in length 14cm. Their food includes earthworms, insects, larvae, seeds and berries. Their melodious song can be heard throughout the year.

Two familiar garden residents, above: Robin, voted Britain's national bird and below: House Sparrow

120

HOUSE SPARROW

Passer domesticus

These birds are closely associated with human habitations and are very seldom seen far from houses and gardens. They were introduced to North America where they have become very numerous. They are almost entirely dependent upon man for their food and only occasionally during autumn and winter will they fly to farmlands in their search for food. Their diet consists of bread, almost all scraps left over from the table and some seed and grain. Both female and male construct an untidy nest of dried vegetation in roofs, holes in trees or hedgerows. The males are distinguished from the females by their black throats and dark grey crowns. They measure in length 14cm. They utter a series of cheeping and chirping notes.

STARLING

Sturnus vulgaris

These birds are partially migratory. Although many north European birds winter in the British Isles, they remain separate from the resident population. Their plumage in the winter becomes speckled, this change being especially noticeable in the females. They measure in length 21cm. They make their nests with dried vegetation and these are usually located in holes in trees or cavities in walls. Their food includes insects, earthworms, seeds, fruit and in the winter scraps of food from the kitchen. When they congregate in their large roosting flocks in city centres their squealing twitters can be heard above the roar of the traffic. They are adept at mimicking the calls and songs of other birds.

Above: Starling
Below: it is rare to see a Swift at rest. So aerial are their habits that their legs have become hardly able to support their weight

SWIFT

Apus apus

They are distinguished from the swallows and martins by their larger size and their scythe-shaped wings, black plumage and short forked tails. They are widespread in towns and cities.

MISTLE THRUSH

Turdus viscivorus

These birds derive their name from their liking of mistletoe berries. They are common in open woodland and parkland and are becoming frequent visitors to gardens in the search for berries. They can be distinguished from the song thrush by their larger size and the large and heavy spots on their underparts. They measure in length 28cm. They construct their large nests between the forks in trees and the nests are made of twigs and grasses and lined with dried mud. Their food includes snails, fruits, berries, seeds, insects and their larvae.

SONG THRUSH

Turdus philomelos

They are very common in parks and gardens and can be distinguished from mistle thrushes and fieldfares by their smaller size. The sexes are similar; they measure in length 23cm. Their nests are made of grasses and lined with dried mud. Their eggs are laid directly on to the mud, whereas the mistle thrush's nest is lined with dried grass. They are well-known for their use of 'anvil' stones for breaking snail shells. They have a preference for certain stones and the area around these is often littered with broken shells. In addition to snails, their food consists of berries, fruit and insects. Their song is heard almost throughout the year and is powerful and melodious.

Above left: juvenile Mistle Thrush
Above and right: Song Thrushes

Left: a Blue Tit makes a landing and below: both parents photographed inside a nest box with their brood

BLUE TIT

Parus caeruleus

These very agile birds with their blue crowns and yellow underparts are very popular in gardens, because they consume large numbers of aphids. In winter and autumn they are familiar visitors to bird-tables and to strings of peanuts and fat hung out for them, but during their breeding season, unless they are using nest-boxes, they prefer open mixed woodlands, where they nest in holes in trees. Their nests are made from dried grass, mosses, lichens and wool. The sexes are similar in appearance; they measure in length 11cm. In addition to aphids, caterpillars, insects and larvae, berries, fruit and some seeds are eaten. Their song is a high pitched 'tsee-tsee'.

123

COAL TIT

Parus ater

They are the smallest of the British tits and are easily distinguishable from blue tits by their drab plumage and the large white patch on the back of their necks. They are shy birds and not so obvious in gardens as blue tits; they prefer coniferous woodlands. The sexes are similar in appearance; they measure in length 10.5cm. Their nests are usually in holes in banks or in rotting tree stumps and are made from hair, mosses and feathers. Their song is a rapid 'seetoo'.

GREAT TIT

Parus major

They are the largest of the British tits and very agile, especially when extracting nuts from containers. Their larger size and the glossy black stripe through their yellow underparts distinguish them from the other tits. The male's black stripe is slightly broader than that of the female. They measure in length 14cm. Often they feed on the ground and, apart from food they take from bird-tables, they consume large numbers of caterpillars, aphids and some fruit and seeds. Their nests are located in holes in trees or cavities in walls and they are made from mosses and hair, and lined with feathers. Their song is a metallic 'teechew-teechew'.

WREN

Troglodytes troglodytes

Only goldcrests are smaller of all birds breeding in the British Isles. Although common in surburban gardens, they are not conspicuous because of their habit of concealing their presence by moving with short darting flights along the most dense part of hedgerows and scrubby vegetation. Another characteristic habit of wrens is that during severe winters they huddle together for warmth in nest boxes and cavities in trees and walls. Often, they are referred to affectionally as 'Jenny' wrens. The male birds construct a number of 'false' nests and the females make the final selection. If food is plentiful and readily available, the males will entice other females to occupy the 'false' nests. They build the domed nests of mosses, leaves and grasses and line them with feathers; these may be found in crevices in walls or trees, in ivy, bushes and earth banks. The sexes are similar in appearance; they measure in length 9.5cm. Their food includes insects and their larvae and some seeds. They have a very loud voice for such a small bird and their song consists of a prolonged jingle.

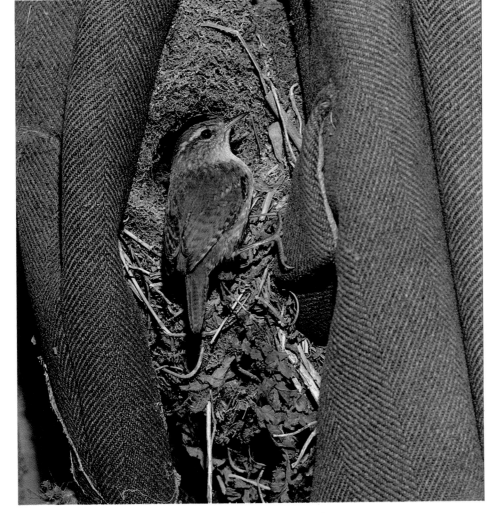

Althoudgh Wrens mostly nest in natural sites (above) the bird on the left has chosen an old jacket in a shed

BIRDS OF THE WOODLANDS

Almost the whole of the woodlands in the British Isles to-day have been planted. There are a few fragments of natural woodland still remaining and one such relic is the Scots pine woodlands at Rothiemurchus, in the Cairngorms National Nature Reserve.

After the retreat of the ice sheets of the last phase of the most recent Ice Age about 8000 years ago, the weather became warmer and wetter and these conditions favoured the spread of broadleaved woodland, in particular oak, birch, ash, elm, hazel and alder. At this time most of these islands became covered with trees apart from the mountain tops and the boggy areas.

Oakwoods are the natural vegetation of the more favourable soils and there are two native oaks, the pedunculate and the sessile. The former is more common in the south and south-east of England and the midlands and the latter has a preference for the more acid soils of the west and north-west of England and Wales. The open structure of the oaks allows a rich herb and shrub layer to develop. Many of the shrubs produce berries which provide food for the thrushes, fieldfares and redwings, and acorns are a favourite food of the jay. Infestations of insect larvae provide food for the smaller woodland birds.

Neolithic man started the destruction of the forests by hacking down and burning the trees on the tops of hills to create land suitable for his crops and grazing for his livestock. This destruction has continued as more and more food is required for an increasing population. By the Middle Ages the forests had been so depleted that timber had to be imported for the construction of ships. The Industrial Revolution brought about a transformation from a mainly agricultural system to one predominantly industrial. This change created even further demands on our limited woodlands for the construction of railways, factories, houses and mining.

During the First World War further inroads were made into the remaining woodlands and as a remedial measure the Forestry Commission was established in 1919. This has increased the acreage of woodlands, but they consist mainly of exotic conifers with some Scots pine in eastern and southern Scotland. Wildlife benefits little from these plantations in their mature stage. During the earlier stages of their growth, however, many birds take advantage of the food and cover they offer, especially the hen harrier.

Typical dense woodland with inset above: the rare Red Kite in flight and below: a female Blackcap

BLACKCAP

Sylvia atricapilla

Although the glossy black caps of the males and the reddish-brown caps of the females are distinctive features of these warblers, it is their rich melodious song which frequently reveals their presence in woodlands. The majority of blackcaps are visitors from Mediterranean countries and Africa. They measure in length 14cm. They frequent woodland with undergrowth and sometimes large gardens with bushes, especially rhododendrons. The fragile nests are made with dried grasses and lined with hair. Their food includes insects, flies, berries and some fruit.

A male Blackcap feeds its young

CAPERCAILLIE

Tetrao urogallus

These very large 'turkey-like' birds of the Scottish pinewoods became extinct during the 18th century and were re-introduced from Swedish stock to Perthshire in the 19th century. Today they are well established and have spread from the Highlands to the Lowlands. Re-introduction has not been successful in Ireland. The males are larger, measuring in length 85cm to the females' 60cm. Their food includes conifer shoots, fruit and berries. The males have a guttural call and the females' is a 'kok-kok'.

A male Capercaillie during a mating display

CHIFFCHAFF

Phylloscopus collybita

These mainly summer migrants are birds of mature woodlands with plenty of undergrowth. Some chiffchaffs remain in southern England and Ireland throughout the winter. Their name is derived from their song, which is a repeated 'chiff-chaff' delivered from tree-tops. This is probably the most satisfactory method of distinguishing the chiffchaffs from the willow warblers, as they are so alike. The sexes are similar in appearance; they measure in length 11cm. Their domed nests are usually located in undergrowth and are made of mosses, dried vegetation and lined with feathers. Their food includes a variety of small insects.

Left: Chiffchaff and below: female Capercaillie

CROSSBILL

Loxio curvirostra

These birds have specially adapted crossed bills to enable them to extract seeds from fir and larch cones, which are their main source of food. The males have crimson plumage, with some brown on the wings and tail feathers, while the females have yellow-green plumage.

129

STOCK DOVE

Columba oenas

These doves are found in a variety of habitats including parks, sparse woodlands, farmland and cliffs. In winter they are often seen feeding with wood pigeons in stubble fields. The sexes are similar in appearance and measure in length 33cm. Their nests are found in a variety of sites including holes in trees, ledges on buildings, under thatches and in rabbit burrows. Their food includes grain, weed seeds, insects and vegetable matter. Their call is a gruff 'ooo-ooo-ooo'.

TURTLE DOVE

Streptopelia turtur

These doves have a preference for thorn thickets, overgrown hedges and bushy woodlands. They are summer visitors and, although widespread in England, they are scarce in Scotland, Ireland and the western counties of Wales. The sexes are similar in appearance; they measure in length 26cm. Their food includes the seeds of weeds, vegetable matter and some invertebrates. Their nests are usually located in trees and large shrubs and are platforms made of twigs. Their song is a purring 'rooor-rooor'.

130

PIED FLYCATCHER

Ficedula hypoleuca

These handsome flycatchers are rather secretive and, hence, have a preference for dense woodland, especially in mid-Wales, although they are increasing their range. The male's pied plumage contrasts with the female's olive-brown colouring. They measure in length 13 cm. Their nests, found in holes in trees or cavities in walls and nest-boxes, are made of leaves, mosses, grasses and rootlets and are sometimes lined with hair or wool. Their food includes mainly flying insects, earthworms and some berries. They have a clear 'whit' call.

Far left above: Turtle Dove; far left centre: Stock Dove and far left below: Pied Flycatcher, beak full of its catch.
Above: two blackcocks confront each other at the 'lek'

GOLDCREST

Regulus regulus

They are the smallest breeding birds in the British Isles and they frequent mixed woodlands. The most distinguishing features are their small size and the males' gold crests.

BLACK GROUSE

Lyrurus tetrix

The males with their distinctive lyre-shaped tails are called blackcocks, and the females greyhens. The males are larger, measuring in length 53cm to the females' 41cm. The males conduct a spectacular communal courtship display at 'leks' (display areas), which are usually located on flat ground on heather moors or fields. Recently, the planting of conifers has produced an increase in their populations both in Scotland and Wales. They are absent from Ireland. Their nests are located on the ground, usually on heather moors or in young conifer plantations. Their food includes conifer, birch and willow shoots, some insects and berries. The males give out a cooing song during their displays at the lek.

JAY

Garrulus glandarius

Although these colourful birds are mainly inhabitants of woodland, they are increasingly found in suburban gardens, especially when peanuts are available. They have a squirrel-like habit of burying acorns during the summer and returning to this source of food during lean periods in the winter. The sexes are similar in appearance; they measure in length 34cm. Their nests are usually located in trees, though they sometimes use tall bushes, are made of twigs and are lined with rootlets and hair. Their food includes vegetative matter, insects and their larvae, young birds and eggs and occasionally mice and voles. Their call is a harsh penetrating 'skraak'.

RED KITE

Milvus milvus

These very rare birds are readily identified when in flight by their deeply forked tail. In the past they were widespread, but are now confined to a small area in central Wales. They are very economical fliers and remain in the air for hours circling above the sparsely wooded hillsides and valleys. The males are smaller, measuring in length 56cm to the females' 61cm. Their nests are located in trees and sometimes they use old crows' nests. Their food includes carrion, rabbits, small birds and frogs. They have a mewing call very similar to that of buzzards, which often occupy the same territory.

Left: a fledgling Jay and above: an adult with the full distinctive plumage

HAWFINCH

Coccothraustes coccothraustes

The most distinguishing features of these uncommon birds are their large bills and thick necks. They have red-brown heads, black throat-patches and red-brown underparts. They frequent mixed or deciduous woodlands.

NIGHTINGALE

Luscinia megarhynchos

These rather inconspicuous birds arrive in spring, the males coming some time before the females. In contradiction to their name they do sing by day. Although their rich and vigorous song is familiar, they are very seldom seen, as their favoured habitat is dense scrubby areas with trees and, in particular, coppiced beech and hornbeam woodlands. The sexes are similar in appearance; they measure in length 16–17cm. Their untidy nests are located in thick undergrowth close to the ground, are made of dead leaves and are lined with grasses and leaves. Their food includes insects and their larvae, and some fruit and berries.

This Nightingale has retained some of its juvenile spots in its plumage. This is most unusual

NIGHTJAR

Caprimulgus europaeus

These summer visitors from Africa have a preference for heathlands and commons, but they breed in mixed woodlands or on bracken covered hillsides. Their colouring produces a very efficient camouflage, as they rest motionless during the day in woodland debris. They feed at dusk on insects, which they catch in flight. When flying, the males' white spots on their wing-tips are visible, but they are absent from the females' wing-tips. They measure in length 27cm. Their call is a soft 'coo-ic'.

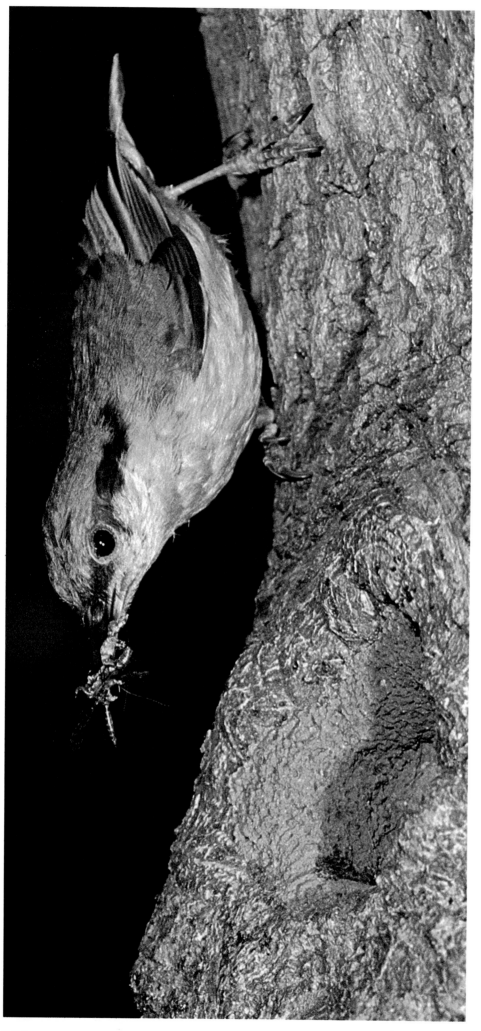

NUTHATCH

Sitta eurapaea

These distinctive dumpy and colourful birds derive their name from the method they use to split nuts. They wedge the nuts in crevices in tree trunks and then attack the nut with their stout bills. They are birds of mature woodlands and are very adept at avoiding obstructions when flying through dense canopies to their nest-holes. They also descend tree-trunks head first. They are seen frequently in parklands and will feed from bird tables in gardens, in particular during the winter months. They are very rare in Scotland and absent from Ireland. The sexes are similar in appearance; they measure in length 14cm. Their nests are located in holes in trees and are made of tree bark and lined with dead leaves; they plaster the entrance to deter larger birds using the nesting hole. Their call is a metallic 'chwit-chwit'. In addition to nuts and seeds their food includes insects and their larvae.

LONG-EARED OWL

Asio otus

These owls are fairly widespread throughout the British Isles apart from south Wales, the Midlands and the extreme south-west of England. Their name is derived from the long erect feathers on the head which resemble ears. The sexes are similar in appearance; they measure in length 35cm. They are nocturnal. Their food includes voles, long-tailed field mice, rats, some birds and insects. They have a preference for using other birds' abandoned nests, while sometimes they will nest on the ground. They have a moaning hooting call.

LESSER REDPOLL

Acanthis flammea

These attractive small birds are increasing in numbers and are widely distributed throughout the British Isles, apart from some south midland counties and the extreme south-west of England. They have a preference for open woodlands of birch and alder and especially conifer plantations. The males have a pinkish flush on their breasts during the breeding season. They measure in length 13cm. Their nests are located in trees or bushes and are made of twigs and feathers. Their food includes seeds, and some insects and larvae. They have a very high-pitched flight call.

Far left: the Nuthatch is the only British bird which habitually climbs downwards on trees.
Above: Nuthatch about to land
Left: Lesser Redpoll. These birds usually sing in flight

REDSTART

Phoenicurus phoenicurus

These handsome visitors from Africa are fairly widespread throughout Britain, although there has been a decline in eastern England, and they are rare in Ireland. Both the males and females have the distinctive red tail, but the males can be identified by their black faces and throats. They measure in length 16cm. They have a preference for woodlands, parklands with trees, gardens with bushes and in the north, areas with dry stone walls. Their nests are usually located in holes in trees, in walls or old buildings, and are made of dried vegetation and lined with hair. Their food includes insects and their larvae, spiders and some berries. Their call is a loud 'weet-tuk-tuk'.

SISKIN

Carduelis spinus

These finches have a preference for coniferous woodlands. They are yellow-green with black crests and streaks of brown on their backs and sides. The females have less prominent yellow colouring.

Above: male Redstart
Right: Tree Sparrow

TREE SPARROW

Passer montanus

These birds have undergone
fluctuations in population for
reasons not yet understood. In
Ireland they were well
established in the last century,
but have since decreased to such
an extent as to have become
rarities. However, there are
signs of a resurgence during the
last decade; there is evidence
that they are also spreading in
Wales and the south of England.
Although they are associated
with mature trees, they do not
always use trees for nesting, but
will use holes in walls, cliffs and
quarries. The nests are made of
dried vegetation and lined with
feathers. The sexes are similar in
appearance and they measure in
length 14cm. Their food includes
seeds and some insects and their
larvae. They have a metallic
'chip-chup' call.

SPARROWHAWK

Accipiter nisus

These birds have been
persistently persecuted by
gamekeepers and farmers for
many years, and another
probable cause of their decline
has been the accumulative effect
of eating birds which had
themselves eaten food
contaminated with pesticides.
Legal protection was granted in
the mid-1960s, and this has
halted their decline; there are
signs that their numbers are now
on the increase. The males are
smaller, measuring in length
27cm, and the females 37cm in
length. They feed mainly on
small birds and some small
mammals, the larger female
occasionally taking birds as big
as pigeons. Their flat nests are
built in trees, usually birch, oak
and larch, and made of twigs.
Their call is a 'kek-kek-kek'.

*Above: female Sparrowhawk on the nest
and a male in flight*

CRESTED TIT

Parus cristatus

These delightful small birds are almost entirely confined to the remnants of the Old Caledonian Pine Forest, although there are signs of the species expanding slowly. Their slender and pointed bills are ideally suited to prising insects and their larvae from amongst pine needles, and they also eat some seeds and berries. Their nests are usually located in holes in tree stumps and are made with mosses, hair, sheep's wool and feathers. The sexes are similar in appearance; they measure in length 11.5–12cm. Their call is different from those of other tits as it is a deep-toned 'choo-rr'.

Above Right: Crested Tit
Right: Marsh Tit
Far right above: Long-tailed Tit at nest
Far right: Willow Tit

LONG-TAILED TIT

Aegithalos caudatus

These attractive and inquisitive birds are found in most types of woodlands and wooded parks, but seldom in suburban gardens. Their elaborate domed nests are the result of both parents working tirelessly for about four weeks prior to egg-laying. The nests are made of a mixture of materials, including lichens, mosses, hair, wool and cobwebs, and are usually located in trees, brambles or bushes. The sexes are similar in appearance; their prominent tails being longer than their bodies, and they measure in total length 14cm. Their food includes insects and their larvae and some seeds. Their call is a low 'tupp' and a 'see-see-see'.

MARSH TIT

Parus palustris

WILLOW TIT

Parus montanus

These birds are associated with mixed woodlands, especially those containing some willows. They are so similar to marsh tits in appearance that the best method of distinguishing between them is by their different calls. The willow tits' call is a grating 'tchay' and sometimes a 'si-si-si', while marsh tits have a 'chick-a-dee' call often followed by a 'pee' note. Their nests are usually located in holes in rotted tree-stumps and are made of mosses, hair, dried grasses and feathers. The sexes are similar in appearance; they measure in length 11.5cm. Their food includes insects and their larvae and some seeds. They are absent from Ireland and northern Scotland.

TREECREEPER

Certhia familiaris

It is surprising that these inhabitants of all types of woodlands throughout the British Isles are seldom seen, as they are not timid and, when approached, will carry on ascending their selected tree quite unconcerned by human presence. In winter, they make use of the deep crevices in the bark of trees like parkland wellingtonias or willows as protection against the cold winds. The sexes are similar in appearance; they measure in length 12–13cm. They nest in tree cavities, holes in walls and sometimes in nest-boxes, but typically behind bark and ivy. The nests are made of dried vegetation and lined with feathers and may contain some bark fragments. Their food includes spiders, caterpillars, grubs, woodlice and some seeds. Their call is a long, high-pitched 'tseee-tseee'.

GARDEN WARBLER

Sylvia borin

Very secretive, they frequent open woodland with a dense cover of brambles and briars. Their nests, usually found in brambles and shrubberies, are flimsy structures mainly of grasses, lined with hair and finer grasses. The sexes are similar in appearance and they measure in length 14 cm. Their food comprises chiefly insects, spiders and some berries and fruit. Their song is a melodious warble and they have a 'tacc-tacc' call when alarmed. They winter in Africa.

WILLOW WARBLER

Phylloscopus trochilus

These summer visitors range throughout the British Isles and are found in all types of woodlands with bushes, on heaths and commons, and in large gardens with trees and shrubs. The sexes are similar in appearance; they measure in length 11cm. They nest on the ground and their nests are made of dried vegetation, mosses and lined with feathers. Their food includes insects and their larvae and some earthworms. Their call is a 'hoo-eet' in two distinct syllables.

WOOD WARBLER

Phylloscopus sibilatrix

These visitors from Africa are usually seen and heard in high tree-tops, where they find their main food of insects and their larvae. Although fairly widespread throughout most counties of England, Scotland and Wales, they are rare in East Anglia and parts of north-east Scotland and are absent from Ireland. The sexes are similar in appearance; they measure in length 12–13cm. Their nests are located on the ground or in scant undergrowth in oak, beech and birch woodlands and are made from dried vegetation and lined with hair. They have a soft 'pu-pu' call.

Far left above: Treecreeper
Far left below: Garden Warbler
Above centre: Willow Warbler
Left: a Wood Warbler clears droppings from the nest and above: hide used to photograph the nest

WAXWING

Bombycilla garrulus

They are winter visitors from
northern Europe usually
arriving in October. They have a
preference for coniferous
woodlands, but are occasionally
found in mixed woodlands,
especially if rowan trees and
other berry-bearing trees and
shrubs are present. In addition to
berries their food includes insects
which are often taken in flight.
The sexes are similar in
appearance and they measure in
length 19cm. They breed in
Scandinavia mainly in conifer
trees and their nests are made
with twigs, grasses and mosses.
They have a rather weak 'shreee'
call.

Waxwing

GREAT-
SPOTTED
WOODPECKER

Dendrocopus major

These are the most widely
distributed of the three resident
woodpeckers, but are rarely
recorded in Ireland. They are
associated with both conifer and
deciduous woodlands and, unlike
the green woodpecker, they very
seldom feed on the ground,
although they will take food from
bird-tables. The males have a
crimson patch on their napes,
which is absent on the females.
They measure in length 23cm.
Their food includes beetles,
wasps and their grubs, moths
nestlings and some vegetable
matter. Their call is a rapid
'chip', but a more characteristic
noise is the resounding
'drum-like' noise they make with
their strong bills on dead trees.

*Great-spotted Woodpecker with food
at nest-hole*

GREEN WOODPECKER

Picus viridis

They are the largest of our three resident woodpeckers and, although their numbers have suffered because of severe winters, they are spreading northwards. They are absent from Ireland. They are found in all types of woodland but have a preference for deciduous trees and especially those in parklands and very large gardens. They can often be observed probing into lawns for their favourite food of ants. They measure in length 32cm. The males have a red centre to a black moustachial stripe which is absent on the females. They nest in holes in trees, their nests consisting mainly of wood chippings. Their food includes, in addition to ants, wood-boring beetles and their larvae. They are called 'yaffles' in many areas because of their 'laughter-like' call.

LESSER SPOTTED WOODPECKER

Dendrocopos minor

They are the smallest of the British woodpeckers, measuring only 14.5cm and they have distinctive black and white barred plumage. The males have red-brown crowns and the females' crowns are off-white.

WRYNECK

Jynx torquilla

These mainly summer visitors from Scandinavia were once found in most English counties, but are now confined to the woodlands of the extreme south-east of England. Their name is derived from their habit of twisting their necks. They breed in holes in trees.

Green Woodpecker

BIRDS' ANCESTORS

Approximately 145,000,000 years ago in the late Jurassic Period, a feathered creature met death in an inland sea and its skeletal remains were impressed between layers of fine-grained limestone. In 1861 quarry-men at Solnhofen in Bavaria, who extracted the limestone for lithographic printing processes, made the most important find in avian history, a fossilised feather. In the same year in a nearby quarry, a fossil skeleton of almost a complete creature was found. The feathers were clearly visible; the creature was obviously a bird, although closely related to reptiles. It was about the same size as a magpie; the jaws contained teeth; it had a long reptilian tail and strong curved claws attached to its wing-tips or fingers. It was given the name *Archaeopteryx lithographica*, the genus name Archaeopteryx meaning 'ancient wing'. Although it had feathered wings, flying requires powerful wing muscles and it did not have a deep keel on the sternum, as modern birds do. So the development of the flight muscles would have been inadequate for long sustained flight. However, its claws would have enabled the bird to climb trees and use the higher branches as launching platforms. One of the five fossil specimens found at Solnhofen may be seen at the Natural History Museum in Kensington.

At the same time, the flying reptiles or pterosaurs shared the same environment as archaeopteryx, and many of their fossil remains have been found at Solnhofen, including pterodactyls. The flying reptiles became extinct by the end of the Cretaceous Period, 65,000,000 years ago. Another bird which became extinct about the same time was the hesperornis (western bird), which lived on the open seas about 100,000,000 years ago. These fish-eating birds had short wings and their legs were so far back on their bodies that they could only have been used as paddles. They were similar in shape to the present-day great northern divers, but much larger, measuring about 2 metres.

Many birds have forsaken their ability to fly and have evolved a flightless life on the ground, especially on remote islands with no natural predators. Unfortunately, when man arrived his immediate impact brought about the extinction of many such birds, including the Mauritian dodo, New Zealand's giant moa and more recently the great auk. Remains of two flightless birds, gastornis and dasornis of the Lower Eocene Period, 55,000,000 years ago, were found in south-eastern England. The fossil remains of an albatross of the Pliocene Period, about 6,000,000 years ago were found in Norfolk. Fragments of the fossil remains of water birds and birds of prey have been found in these islands from the Pleistocene Period, 1,000,000 years onwards. The fossil remains of birds are a rarity, as their bones are light and hollow and, therefore, are not easily preserved. The fortunate find of archaeopteryx at Solnhofen has enabled many interesting theories to be developed regarding the beginnings of birds. It is hoped, however, that with improved digging techniques, further fossil remains will be forthcoming. With the convergence of evidence, a better understanding of bird evolution will result.

A reconstruction of Archaeopteryx. By permission of the Trustees of the British Museum (Natural History)

The Photographers

The numbers refer to the page each photograph appears on: the letters refer to the sequence on that page, reading left to right and top to bottom.

11*c*, 15, 23*a*, 26*b*, 28*b*, 43*b*, 64*b*, 98*a*,

HOWARD GINN M.A., (Cantab), A.R.P.S., is employed by the Nature Conservancy Council. He is an adviser to the Government on matters related to bird conservation. He is Deputy Chairman of the Natural History Group of the Royal Photographic Society. He was formerly with the British Trust for Ornithology, where he was responsible for the research programmes into bird moulting and the compilation of the results of bird-ringing. Although he is interested in all types of bird photography, he has a preference for flight photography.

He uses a Canon camera, with motor drive and Novaflex 400mm and 600mm telephoto lenses.

11*a*, 35, 60*a*, 83*b*, 96*a*, 130*a*, 142*a*

FRANK GREENAWAY is employed by the British Museum (Natural History), Kensington as a photographer. Although his photography involves considerable travelling throughout Britain, he has a preference for the isolated islands, such as Ailsa Craig, Bass Rock and Puffin Island, where he photographs sea-cliff birds. His work on kingfishers in collaboration with Alan Shears is well known.

He uses Hasselblad and Nikon cameras with a range of lenses.

11*b*, 19*a*, 23*b*, 38, 40*b*, 41, 42*b*, 42*c*, 43*c*, 49*b*, 58*b*, 63*a*, 68*b*, 70*b*, 74, 75*b*, 80*a*, 84*a*, 84*b*, 85*b*, 91*b*, 92*b*, 102*a*, 121*a*, 121*b*

GEOFFREY KINNS, naturalist, wildlife photographer and illustrator, was formerly with the exhibition section of the British Museum (Natural History), Kensington. He is probably better known for his photography of mammals, and his book on *British Wild Animals* was published recently by Hodder and Stoughton. However, he has also an extensive collection of bird photography, especially of birds of prey and waders. He is a familiar sight at Minsmere, Gibraltar Point and the Highlands of Scotland with his array of cameras.

He uses a Hasselblad 500C electrically-operated camera with a 500mm Tessar telephoto lens; also he uses a Nikon camera with a 560mm Telyt telephoto lens.

24*a*, 24*b*, 25*a*, 29, 32 *main illus*, 37*a*, 44*a*, 46 *main illus*, 51*a*, 51*b*, 53*b*, 55*b*, 56 *main illus*, 56*b*, 65*a*, 70*a*, 72 *main 44a, 46 main illus*, 51*a*, 51*b*, 55*b*, 56 *main illus*, 56*b*, 65*a*, 70*a*, 72 *main illus*, 78*a*, 80*b*, 82, 94*c*, 95*a*, 98 *main illus*, 100*b*, 103*a*, 104*a*, 104*b*, 107*b*, 108*b*, 110 *main illus*, 110*a*, 113*a*, 117, 119*a*, 122*b*, 124*b*, 125*a*, 128*a*, 129*a*, 130*c*, 133*a*, 134, 136*a*, 139*a*, 140*a*, 140*b*, 141*b*, 141*c*

ERIC HERBERT, mountaineer and bird photographer, was formerly with the British Museum (Natural History), Kensington, as an exhibition designer and organiser. His climbing experience and skills have enabled him to specialise in the photography of sea-cliff birds in otherwise inaccessible situations. However, he has not confined his photography to the inhabitants of precipitous sea-cliffs and his excellent photography of kingfishers and long-tailed tits exemplifies his versatility and skill. Recently, he has undertaken the conservation management of a private lake, in an endeavour to increase the varieties and population of wildfowl.

He uses a Mamiyaflex C2 body with a 110 Sekor standard lens, 180mm Sekor telephoto lens and a 250mm Sekor telephoto lens. His 35mm photography is taken with a Pentax ME automatic camera with 50mm standard lens and a 200mm telephoto lens.

BOB LAMBIE is employed by British Rail in Glasgow. The appeal of the Scottish Highlands is reflected in his photography of species indigenous to the beautiful and sometimes hostile environment. He is a member of the Scottish Ornithologists' Club and also of the Royal Society for the Protection of Birds. He enjoys lecturing on the birds of the Scottish Highlands to the Scottish Wildlife Trust members, outdoor clubs and Women's Guilds.

He uses a Practika LTL camera with a Taunton 300mm telephoto lens.

DON MacGASKILL has been with the Forestry Commission in Perthshire for over 30 years and during this time has become aware of the needs for conservation of the wildlife of the Scottish woodlands. This deep interest in the survival of wildlife has resulted in his excellent photographic records of the many indigenous plants, mammals and birds of the forests.

He uses a Nikon camera with 400mm–500mm lenses.

A. SHEARS is an electrical engineer and is employed by the Redhill General Hospital. Originally, bird photography was a means of relaxation, but it was not long before he began to apply his considerable electronic skills to photography. He has designed and constructed infra-red equipment for triggering the camera shutter. Now he is developing a flash-gun capable of operating at 1/25,000 of a second.

He uses Mamiyaflex cameras with 180mm and 300mm Sekor lenses, and a Hasselblad 500C, with 80mm, 150mm and 250mm telephoto lenses.

WOLFGANG WAGNER, architectural designer and traveller, specialises in the photography of birds of prey, which he photographs in Britain, Turkey and Japan. Although his birds of prey photography is well-known on the Continent, this is the first time his work has appeared in a British publication. He is also an excellent plant photographer.

He uses a Canon F1 camera with motor-drive and 400mm–600mm Novaflex telephoto lenses.

JOHN WATKINS is a commodity broker in the City of London – he began photographing birds as a relaxation after a week in the City. He has been taking bird photographs for fifteen years and he has a definite preference for photographing falcons and owls. His photograph of the kestrel which appears in this book demanded considerable patience to achieve, a vigil of over 50 hours being necessary to obtain this excellent picture. Recently, he has been concentrating on flight photography of passerines. He is a member of the Rye Meads bird ringing society.

He uses Pentax and Olympus cameras with 200mm lenses for nest photography and 400mm lenses for photographing wading birds.

Other photographers whose work appears in this book:

Organisations concerned with the protection of birds and the countryside

BRITISH TRUST FOR ORNITHOLOGY

The British Trust for Ornithology was formed in 1933 to harness the scientific potential to be obtained from co-operation with amateur ornithologists. The founders of the Trust considered that if the many enthusiastic bird-watchers would collaborate on fundamental investigations, information could be acquired that had not been possible previously. Also, they believed that many bird-watchers would prefer to be organised so that the maximum benefit would be derived from their field observations. Their conjecture proved to be correct and, now, a host of birdwatchers, its numbers increasing continually, still supports this fundamental concept. It remains the basis of the Trust's work. The traditional type of investigations carried out by the BTO still remains to-day as it developed in its early days. They originate from ideas suggested by members, and are organised by the members. The facts resulting from the national network of observers are collated and reports are produced. Some of these surveys were initiated some time ago; for example the Census of Heronries, which began in 1928, was taken over by the Trust when it was founded and has continued every year since. The great crested grebe survey of the species distribution is another long-term inquiry, which began in 1935, and was repeated each year from 1946–1955 and again in 1965.

The Trust has conducted surveys into the breeding distribution of common birds, which include the mute swan, and of the rarer species such as the firecrest. Other investigations have included the wintering of gulls, the migration of wood pigeons, the roosting habits of starlings, the opening of milk bottle tops by tits, the mortality of birds on the roads and many others. More recent surveys have been the distribution of Britain's rookeries, the breeding birds of waterways and the relative importance of the nightingale.

Many of their investigations have provided essential information to conservation. Others, notably the peregrine falcon survey, have revealed valuable information regarding the effects of pesticides. A recent project, the Register of Ornithological Sites, has as its main aim the provision of information for conservation objectives.

Other activities that are being planned for action are the censuses of the peregrine falcon and the nightjar and participation in a *European Breeding Atlas* commencing in 1985. Consideration is being given to work on a sample basis of bird populations on permanent meadows.

The success of the BTO's *Atlas of Breeding Birds in Britain and Ireland*, which had contributions from over 8000 birdwatchers, gained enormously from the observers' local knowledge.

The Trust maintains close links with local ornithology through its network of Regional Representatives, joint meetings with county societies and regional conferences.

Members of the Trust are encouraged to co-operate with ornithologists of other European countries. Officers of the Trust act as secretaries and chairmen to European committees for co-ordinating ringing, census studies, atlas projects and wading bird studies.

The Trust provides opportunities for birdwatchers to meet, and holds a number of conferences each year. It publishes a scientific journal, *Bird Study*, a bulletin, *BTO News* and booklets on many different subjects related to the ever-changing status of birds.

Members become well-informed partners in a body of enthusiasts devoted to the study and care of birds.

British Trust for Ornithology. Beech Grove, Tring, Hertfordshire, HP23 5NR.

An expert rings a Black-headed Gull. Anyone finding a ringed bird should inform the British Museum (Natural History) London SW7 5BD noting where and when the bird was found, its state of health and the number on the ring

INTERNATIONAL COUNCIL FOR BIRD PRESERVATION

It was not until the early 1920s that the idea of an international organisation for bird protection was formed, when in 1922 Dr T. Gilbert Pearson, President of the National Association of Audubon Societies in the USA, made an extensive tour of Europe. He found that little was known about bird protection activities in the USA and that no country in Europe had more than a limited knowledge of what their neighbouring countries were doing. As a result Dr Pearson, on June 22nd 1922, invited a group of people who met at the home of Mrs Reginald McKenna, wife of the then Chancellor of the Exchequer. They included Earl Buxton, Viscount Grey of Falloden and Dr Percy Lowe of Great Britain, Dr P. G. van Tienhoven and Dr W. Burdet of Holland and Jean Delacour of France and, at this meeting, the International Committee for Bird Preservation was founded. In 1958 the title of the ICBP was changed from Committee to Council, thus reflecting the high international standing it had achieved.

The strength of the ICBP lies with its National Sections. They act as focal points for national opinion in each country and as channels for co-operation in matters of international concern. The ICBP is a non-governmental and entirely independent body. Each National Section has its own constitution, but some Sections are supported by their governments. The British National Section is a registered charity depending for funds on private and public donations.

The ICBP has achieved many successful projects but none greater than the promotion of international approaches to bird preservation by showing that migratory birds do not belong to one country, but to many countries. At the ICBP meeting in Sweden in 1950, a scheme was designed for the creation of reserves along the European migratory routes, and since that meeting further progress has been achieved in co-operation with other international organisations.

In 1960, during the ICBP meeting in Japan, an Asian Continental Section was established with the protection of migratory birds in the Pan-Pacific area as the highest priority. This resulted in the USA/Japan Convention for the Protection of Migratory Birds and their Environment and Birds in Danger of Extinction, which in turn was followed by a similar agreement between Japan and the USSR and Japan and Australia.

Since its inception the ICBP has recognised and waged battle against such universal dangers as oil pollution of the seas, uncontrolled use of toxic chemicals, the draining of wetlands and the indiscriminate shooting of wildfowl. The problem of sea pollution by oil discharges was started by the change-over from coal-burning to oil-burning ships. As this practice spread, thousands of sea-birds were annually destroyed and, although measures were taken to control the discharge of waste oil into the sea and the matter was taken up by the League of Nations, nothing practical was achieved. In 1952, on the initiative of the British Section of the ICBP, the Advisory Committee of Oil Pollution of the Sea (ACOPS) was set up under the chairmanship of Mr James Callaghan. The outcome was an international conference organised in London. This conference was followed in 1954 by an Inter-Governmental Conference convened by the UK, at which an international convention was drawn up containing many measures to contain oil pollution. The ICBP and ACOPS continue to work to prohibit waste oil discharges into the sea and ensure a future for sea-birds. In 1960, a referendum organised by the ICBP and supported by *The Times* resulted in the robin being elected as Britain's National Bird. Today the ICBP has 61 National Sections in every continent of the world. *Birds International* is the ICBP's quarterly magazine which provides members with information and a degree of involvement in the work of the Council.

International Council for Bird Preservation. 219c Huntingdon Road, Cambridge, CB3 0DL

IRISH WILDBIRD CONSERVANCY

The Irish Wildbird Conservancy was founded in 1969 by the amalgamation of three other ornithological societies. Its aims are conservation, education and research in relation to wild birds in Ireland.

In the early years of this century the chief threats to wild birds came from overshooting and egg-stealing. Several birds of prey became extinct in Ireland as a result and early efforts were directed towards the protection of rare breeding species. In recent decades with the rapid modernisation of Irish agriculture the most serious threats have become those affecting the habitats of birds. Major arterial drainage schemes are changing the character of whole river basins. Reclamation of marginal land is threatening coastal lakes and estuaries. Several large midland lakes are seriously polluted by sewage and farm effluent.

The search for fuel has led to the development of more and more small bogs. Each year more deciduous woodland falls victim to the chainsaw only to be replaced by monstrous ranks of conifer plantations. If the present rate of habitat destruction continues more wildlife species will certainly become extinct in Ireland.

One of the most urgent tasks of the IWC is therefore the establishment of reserves to protect the more sensitive species. The Wexford Wildfowl Reserve is jointly owned by the IWC and the Irish Government to protect a large proportion of the world population of Greenland white-fronted geese each winter. Other IWC reserves include Little Skellig, which holds 20,000 pairs of gannets and Puffin Island with a major colony of Manx shearwaters and puffins.

IWC members take an active part in national surveys which provide the information on which the conservation effort is based. The *Atlas of Breeding Birds in Britain and Ireland* (1976) and the recent *Atlas of Winter Birds in Britain and Ireland* were both undertaken jointly with the British Trust for Ornithology.

Ireland's wintering wildfowl and waders were the subject of an extensive IWC Wetlands Enquiry 1971–75 which resulted in the IWC publication *Ireland's Wetlands and their Birds* (1979). Information on important habitats for birds is supplied to local authorities for inclusion in their development plans. Where thoughtless developments do threaten bird haunts they are actively opposed through planning appeals. Cases of infringement of the Wildlife Act 1976 are brought to the attention of the authorities and prosecution of offenders is encouraged as an example to others.

Hand in hand with thse activities goes an expanding educational programme for both schools and the general public. Annual field courses are enormously popular and two highly-acclaimed films have been produced. IWC publications include an annual journal, *Irish Birds*, and local bird guides.

The IWC has a fast-growing membership which is kept in touch through the medium of a quarterly newsletter, always packed with photographs, information and articles on birds and other wildlife. Two annual conferences are held, one jointly with the RSPB in Northern Ireland. There are nine IWC branches around the country which provide enjoyable outings, film shows and lectures for the more active members.

Until recently all the work of the IWC was done in a voluntary capacity but a full-time Director was appointed in 1980 and an office headquarters established. The conservation of Irish birds is a daunting task but the IWC as a growing voluntary organisation is well placed to meet the challenge.

Irish Wildbird Conservancy. Southview, Church Road, Greystones, Co. Wicklow.

NATURE CONSERVANCY COUNCIL

The Nature Conservancy Council was established by the Nature Conservancy Council Act, 1973, and was derived from the Nature Conservancy created in 1949. It is responsible for promoting the conservation of flora, fauna, geological and physiographical features throughout England, Scotland and Wales. Similar responsibility in Northern Ireland is administered by the Northern Ireland Department of the Environment, advised by the Nature Reserves Committee.

The Nature Conservancy Council is financed by the Department of the Environment. However, the Council is free to express independent views; for example, it opposes the granting of planning permission if it considers that development would be damaging to nature conservation. The Council establishes, maintains and manages National Nature Reserves, of which there are now 173, covering nearly 134,485 hectares (332,320 acres). A recent acquisition worthy of note has been the 2200 hectares (5450 acres) of salt-marsh and tidal-flats in the Ribble estuary, Lancashire, an internationally important site for waterfowl, which the Council acquired in 1979 in spite of plans to embank and drain the area for more intensive agriculture. The management of nature reserves covers a range of activities, particularly the protection, and occasionally the creation, of wildlife habitats and the promotion of research, interpretation and education.

The Council also undertakes surveys to identify areas of special scientific importance for nature conservation. In 1977, 735 key sites were identified as containing sufficient scientific merit to be of National Nature Reserve status.

The Council has a statutory duty to advise local planning authorities of any area which it considers to be of special biological, geological or physiographical interest. More than 3700 such 'sites of special scientific interest' have been notified to the authorities. The planning authorities must consult the Council before granting planning permission for change of land use.

The Council has the responsibility of advising the Government on nature conservation policies and the effect other policies may have on nature conservation. The Council carries out research, either through its own specialist staff or commissioned from other agencies and individuals, especially from the Natural Environment Research Council. Also, the Council gives grants for nature conservation projects, including grants towards the purchase of nature reserves, equipment and vehicles to enable groups to undertake nature conservation and management.

The Council is conducting a most interesting experiment on the Isle of Rhum National Nature Reserve by the re-introduction of the Sea Eagle (*Haliaetus albicilla*) from Norway where the species is protected and some 400 pairs still breed. A previous re-introduction experiment was unsuccessful on Fair Isle, but it is hoped that, the Isle of Rhum being larger, this experiment will succeed.

Most British birds are protected but can be photographed at any time. The 86 rare breeding species listed on Schedule 1 of the Wildlife and Countryside Act 1981 can only legally be photographed during the breeding season, from nest-building to independence of the young (unless they are away from their nests or dependent young), under licence. Such licences may be granted to experienced workers of proven skill by the Nature Conservancy Council, address below. For certain very rare species, no photography is allowed or only in certain stronghold areas. Early application from November to January is recommended.

Nature Conservancy Council, Great Britain Headquarters.
Northminster House, Peterborough, PE1 1UA

ROYAL SOCIETY FOR THE PROTECTION OF BIRDS

The Society was founded in 1889 to protest against a flourishing trade in birds' feathers for millinery. It was not long before its growing status merited the granting of a Royal Charter in 1904 and to-day it boasts 350,000 adult and over 100,000 junior members of the Young Ornithologists Club, the largest youth wildlife club in the world.

The primary aim of the Society was to achieve effective legislation to protect wild birds, but this concept was soon expanded as other threats to bird life were recognised. The acquisition of reserves, to be managed by the Society's staff, for the provision and protection of habitat has become a prime object. This will remain so, as loss of habitat is undoubtedly the greatest single threat to bird life. Today the Society currently manages ninety reserves throughout Great Britain. Another threat is the continuing problem of pollution, whether from oil spills at sea, factory effluent in rivers or chemical pesticides on land. RSPB research programmes seek workable solutions to these and other problems as they are recognised. Because birds are vulnerable to the many pressures imposed by the encroaching presence of man in the countryside, the Society has a unit which is proving increasingly successful in prosecuting nest-robbers and egg-stealers. An army of helpers during the breeding season maintains a round-the-clock watch on the nests of our rarer birds to try and ensure that they fledge their young without human disturbance or predation. Constantly vigilant in considering plans for development or alterations in land use, the Society has successfully opposed proposals in various parts of the country which were deemed to pose an unacceptable threat to bird life. Much, too, continues to be done in the legislative field. The RSPB's work is publicised by an active programme of education, both for schools and teachers, and by exhibitions and displays. Magazines are produced for both adults and for YOC members. Films made by the RSPB's own film unit are shown throughout the country, and are also shown on television and sold abroad, where they have won the highest awards.

Nine regional offices, including an office each in Scotland, Wales and Northern Ireland, ensure that the Society's work is developed on a nationwide basis. Influence in the international field has expanded considerably in recent years and the Society's views are widely respected. Members are encouraged to take an active part in events by joining one of the members' groups, serviced from headquarters but conducted by local committees. A flourishing trading company sells goods designed to promote an interest in birds and there is an active fund-raising section.

For the future the Society envisages making a practical approach to the problems ahead with a refusal to be sidetracked from the major issues. Whilst holding to clearly defined aims, the intention will continue to be to find solutions through co-operation rather than opposition. One of the tragedies of the modern world is that the needs of man and birds so often prove irreconcilable. The Society believes that a professional outlook offers the best hope for commensense compromise.

Royal Society for the Protection of Birds. The Lodge, Sandy, Bedfordshire, SG19 2DL.

WORLD WILDLIFE FUND

The World Wildlife Fund is an international organisation, based in Switzerland, with twenty-seven national organisations around the world. It was founded in 1961 when many people were becoming seriously alarmed at the rapid decline of wildlife and the destruction of natural habitats.

The concern of the World Wildlife Fund is the natural environment, its animals and plants and the ecological web which binds them together with climate, soil and water into those healthy ecosystems which for centuries mankind has described as Nature. The WWF gives particular attention to endangered species and those which have been seriously depleted by the impact of man, and to endangered natural habitats.

At the same time the WWF is acutely aware of the causal factors which make nature conservation so necessary and urgent – the problem of human population increase, of high technology agriculture, of industrialisation and urbanisation, of pollution, of misuse and waste of resources and energy, and of famine and poverty. If solutions to these problems can be found, the WWF's aims will be more easily achieved, for it is clear that the conservation of nature cannot be accomplished in isolation from the human condition. However, in view of the limited funds available, the WWF's priority projects are mainly, though not exclusively, directed towards wildlife – defined as wild animals and plants and their wild habitats. Between its formation in 1961 and the present time the World Wildlife Fund has channelled over 25 million pounds into more than 2500 projects, which have saved animals from extinction and helped to conserve habitats throughout the world. The tiger, wolf, Asiatic lion, Javan rhinoceros, elephant, Arabian oryx, vicuna, Hawaiian goose, marine turtles and crocodiles are among the species given a new lease of life by the WWF.

Conservation of habitats is vital to the future of wild species. WWF has helped fund 250 national parks and other protected areas in five continents. They cover an area of 1,300,000 square kilometres, which is twice the size of Texas, or equal to France, West Germany, Italy and the United Kingdom combined.

WWF aid has included provision of equipment, such as aircraft, vehicles, binoculars, camping gear and scientific and technical instruments, as well as finance for surveys, preparation of management plans and technical assistance. Among key conservation areas which have received WWF aid are the Serengeti National Park in Tanzania, Manu National Park in Peru, Guning Leuser Reserve in Indonesia, Donana National Park in Spain and the New Jersey wetlands in the United States. At the same time the WWF has used its influence to promote national conservation programmes in countries such as Costa Rica, Nepal and Pakistan, and international legislation, such as the Convention on International Trade in Endangered Species of Wild Fauna and Flora (CITIES), and the International Agreement on Conservation of Polar Bears.

Regular financial support for the International Union for Conservation of Nature and Natural Resources (IUCN) has enabled the organisation to develop and maintain its key role as the world's leading scientific conservation body. The publication of the World Conservation Strategy in 1980, in which the WWF played a major role, has led to even greater attention being given to the need to conserve the world's natural resources. In Britain, the WWF has contributed more than one million pounds to the conservation of threatened animals, plants and habitats. Beech woods, chalk grasslands and marshes are some of the wild places that have been secured for all time.

World Wildlife Fund UK. 11–13 Ockford Road, Godalming, Surrey, GU7 1QU

Acknowledgements

It has been my privilege to gather together the work of the photographers whose photographic skills and ornithological knowledge has enabled this book to be published. In particular, I am most grateful to Eric Herbert, who has worked tirelessly to acquire crucial photographs at very short notice, by his own endeavours or from his wide source of naturalist/photographer friends. Also, I wish to thank David Burton, B.Sc., for giving up some of his holiday to undertake the rather boring task of checking the text, and Will Facey, M.A., F.R.G.S. who read substantial parts of the text and gave me good advice. I owe a great debt of gratitude to Mrs Marion Marsh and Miss Jane Osborn, of the staff of Hodder and Stoughton, for their tolerance and technical and editorial skills. Lastly, to the birds who give me so much pleasure . . . thank you.

Bibliography

BARNES, RICHARD *Coasts and Estuaries* Hodder and Stoughton, 1979.

BOATMAN, DEREK *Fields and Lowlands* Hodder and Stoughton, 1979.

BRAUN, BARTEL *The Hamlyn Guide to the Birds of Britain and Europe* Hamlyn 1970.

BRITISH ORNITHOLOGISTS' UNION *Checklist of the Birds of Great Britain and Ireland* 1952

CRAMP, S.C. AND OTHERS *The Sea Birds* Collins, 1974

DARLINGTON, ARNOLD *Mountains and Moorlands* Hodder and Stoughton, 1979

EVERETT, MICHAEL *The Guiness Book of Woodland Birds* Guiness Superlatives Ltd., 1980

FEDUCCIA, ALAN *The Age of Birds* Harvard University Press, 1980

FISHER, JAMES *Thorburn's Birds (revised edition)* Ebury Press, 1976

HALLIDAY, TIM *Vanishing Birds* Sidgwick and Jackson, 1978

KENNEDY, P.C. AND OTHERS *Birds of Ireland* Oliver and Boyd, 1954

MURTON, R.K. *Birds and Man* Collins, 1971

OWEN, DENNIS *Towns and Gardens* Hodder and Stoughton, 1979

PETERSEN, R. T. AND OTHERS *A Field Guide to the Birds of Britain and Europe* Collins, 1966

The Readers Digest Book of British Birds (3rd edition) Drive Publications Ltd, 1980

SIMS, ERIC *Birds of the Towns and Suburbs* Collins, 1975

SWINNERTON, H. H. *Fossils* Collins, 1960

SWINTON, E. E. *Fossil Birds* (3rd edition) Trustees of the British Museum (Natural History), 1975

WITHERBY, H. F. AND OTHERS *The Handbook of British Birds 5 volumes* H. F. and G. Witherby Ltd, 1938–41

WHITTON, BRIAN *Rivers, Lakes and Marshes* Hodder and Stoughton, 1979

Index of English Names Numbers in bold type refer to photographs

Index of Latin Names Numbers in bold type refer to photographs